W9-CDT-245

CUONG PHAM

WITH TIEN NGUYEN AND DIEP TRAN

THE RED BOAT FISH SAUCE COOKBOOK

BELOVED RECIPES FROM THE FAMILY BEHIND THE PUREST FISH SAUCE

HOUGHTON MIFFLIN HARCOURT
BOSTON NEW YORK 2021

FOR MY MOTHER AND FATHER,
CÁI THỊ KIM VÂN
AND PHẠM TẤN NAM

ACKNOWLEDGMENTS

The journey to launch Red Boat was a deeply personal one, but one I could not have done alone. First and foremost, there is my family: My wife, Ann, and children, Tracy, Kevin, and Tiffany, have been pillars of support. Võ Trần mentored me from the beginning, back when I was going door to door with those ungainly jugs of fish sauce, and I am deeply grateful for his advice throughout the years. Thiệt and Bảo Trần, Peter and Michael Pham, and Sam Luu were part of the Red Boat opening team, and they helped lay our groundwork of distributors and markets. And Betsy Fox helped bring attention to Red Boat from the beginning.

In Việt Nam, my late aunt Phạm Thị Duyên, Thái Thị Túy Liên, and Nguyễn Văn Hiệp helped me establish Red Boat and plowed through mountains of paperwork to make the business a reality. Thank you to Nguyễn Thị Thùy Vân, Phan Trọng Dực, our barrel house manager Trần Thị Ánh Hồng, and Nguyễn Đình Phương, all of whom were critical in building Red Boat in Việt Nam. And an enormous thank you to the crew at our barrel house: Captains Nguyễn Văn Phúc and Nguyễn Vĩnh, Lê Văn Bạc, Nguyễn Thị Tiền, Lê Hoàng Đệ, Trần Thi Thanh Tâm, Phạm Thị Thuỳ Ngân, Nguyễn Thanh Việt, Danh Hồng Lắm, and Nguyễn Hồng Sơn.

Our US crew does everything from bottling to shipping, and we could not do what we do without them. An enormous thank you to Tony Mao, Tony Khauv, Sang Ho, Nhieu Huynh, Thanh Huynh, Tam Huynh, Chris Salcedo, Viet Pham, Nguyễn Đắc Lộ, and Lee Ikegami.

The groundswell of support we have received from our fans is truly overwhelming. To our fans, I am so, so appreciative of your support. Red Boat would not be here without you. In particular, thank you to Hong and Kim Pham, Monique Trương, Florence Fabricant, Cathy Chaplin, Michelle Tam, Andrea Nguyen, Stefan and Simi Leistner, Robert Danhi, Bee Yinn Low, and Lace Zhang for spreading the word in those early days. And a big thanks to Mai Hà and Mai Hoàng Oanh, who were first to stock Red Boat at their store, Nam Hoa Market.

When I started Red Boat, I was thinking of home cooks like my mother. I didn't expect Red Boat would one day be used in restaurants! Thank you to the chef community for embracing our fish sauce; thank you, especially, to Stuart Brioza, Nicole Krasinski, Bryant Ng, Kim Luu-Ng, Braden and Yasmin Wages, Christine Ha, Justin Chao, and Khanh Ngô for being such ardent supporters and for contributing such wonderful recipes to this book. And thank you to Chris Shepherd, Ed Lee, and Chris Cosentino for your support.

Putting together this cookbook—during a pandemic, no less—was a feat. I'd like to thank Michele Crim, our agent, who was so instrumental in pulling the pieces together and was a guiding light as we navigated the book world. Thank you to Hồng, who helped source and prep ingredients in Phú Quốc and managed our grueling photoshoot schedule. Thank you to Nguyễn Thị Thanh Thuý, who took the time to meet and chat with me over bowls of Đào Thị Thanh's fantastic bún riêu, and thank you, Thanh, for your hospitality. Thank you to Lê Thị Kim Điền, who coordinated our trip to the salt fields, giving us a new appreciation of the amount of labor it takes to harvest this precious mineral. Thank you, Oriana Koren, for your stunning photos. The way you captured Việt Nam, our food, and my family is truly special. Jessica Wang was a brilliant prop stylist; thank you, Jess, for your eye and instinct. Thank you, Jules Exum, for your tireless efforts throughout the photoshoot in Việt Nam and in Los Angeles. Celeste Noche, thank you for your prop styling expertise during those humid days in Việt Nam, and for sourcing such beautiful plates, bowls, cups, and flatware. Thank you to Kathy Minh Bạch, who provided guidance for where to source vintage tableware in Sài Gòn. And thank you to Liam Montano, who crafted the distinctive pink table and blue bench we used throughout the shoot back in Los Angeles.

To the entire team at Houghton Mifflin Harcourt: Thank you. Our manuscript was skillfully and thoughtfully edited by Sarah Kwak. We cannot thank you enough, Sarah, for being open to, and honoring, our vision for this book. And big thanks to Melissa Lotfy, our art director, and Sebit Min, our designer: The book is beautiful. We could not have asked for a better copyeditor than Michael Olivo, who ironed out the wrinkles in our text. Thank you to Justin Schwartz, who saw the potential in our book, and Jacqueline Quirk for your assistance throughout this process. And to everyone else at HMH who helped bring our book to life: Thank you, thank you.

A huge thank you to Diep Tran, for being one of the earliest supporters of Red Boat, recreating our family recipes, and turning this cookbook into a reality. We are so grateful to Tien Nguyen for her captivating storytelling in memorializing the Red Boat story.

Finally, my sisters, Điệp and Lan, deserve special recognition. Their memories and cooking skills informed so much of this book, and they provided enormous assistance with developing and testing our family recipes. Thank you.

INTRO DUCTION

I launched Red Boat Fish Sauce in 2011 in northern California, but the true origin story of Red Boat starts decades earlier on an entirely different continent. It starts, really, in Việt Nam, with my mother.

My mother grew up in Rạch Giá, the capital of the Kiên Giang province on the southwestern coast of Việt Nam. Her father (my grandfather) developed land nearby in An Biên—he was so well-known that he was informally considered the mayor of the area. I still have family there, in fact, some still living along the very same road where our ancestral home is located.

My mom's interest in food and cooking began at a very young age. This did not go unnoticed by my grandfather, who embraced her love for all things culinary and arranged for her to receive formal French training in Sài Gòn. It was there her natural talent blossomed, and she became an amazing cook.

My mom eventually moved to Sài Gòn, which is where I grew up. She was a teacher at the grade school just a few steps away from our home, but outside of school, she was always cooking. In fact, her cooking was so well known that our house was a de facto gathering spot where my friends and my siblings' friends would pop by during the holidays or in time for lunch, dinner, or snacks after school. Her Tết (Lunar New Year) spread was legendary: Weeks before the holiday, a relative would drop by with a few liters of fish sauce—and not just any fish sauce, but fish sauce from Phú Quốc island, which was well known then, as it is now, as being home to some of the best fish sauce in the world. With that crucial ingredient delivered, she began prepping. There were carrots and radishes to pickle, lotus roots to slice for salads (page 223), and big pots of my favorite, thịt kho trứng (caramelized pork braise with eggs, page 229) to simmer. And while my mom pulled out all the stops for Tết, the rest of the year was just as delicious as she whipped up things like cháo bồi (a shrimp and crab rice soup, page 218) and nem nướng (grilled pork meatballs, page 149).

In retrospect, I realize I took the great food that came out of her kitchen for granted. I didn't consider how she managed to feed us six kids after the end of the war in 1975. I took what seemed like an unlimited supply of beautiful fish sauce for granted, too. In my youth, I couldn't have fathomed the ways in which the war, global consumer demand, and intense competition would radically change the fish sauce industry in the decades to come.

Four years after the end of the war, my mother made a monumentally difficult decision: It was time to leave Việt Nam and find a better future elsewhere. My mom decided we would all go, but to be safe, we'd go separately. I'd be the first in the family to go.

In February 1979, just a few days after Tết, I set out. The plan was for me to hide out on a designated fishing boat, wait for my other siblings to join me, and then, hopefully, we'd all ship out. For two weeks, I hid and waited, hid and waited; meanwhile, the boat was a destination for others, too, and as the days passed, it filled with more and more people following their own plans of escape. None of my siblings turned up though, and after about two weeks, we got word that some people were getting caught on their way to the boat. No longer safe to wait, we lurched into the water. Including the time I spent in a refugee camp in Pulau Bidong in Malaysia—which was being used exclusively as a camp for refugees— it was nine months before I finally touched ground in the United States. I was twenty years old.

As it turns out, I was the first in my family to leave Việt Nam, but not the first to arrive in the US. Two brothers arrived in the States before I did; I briefly stayed with one in Boston before joining my other brother in the Bay Area. There I earned my degree in management information systems and, in 1984, landed a job as a systems engineer for a guy named Steve Jobs at what was then his small computer company, Apple.

I started right around the storied launch of its Macintosh computer and wound up staying for over a decade. Steve was ousted from the company just a year after I arrived, but in that short period of time, I learned so much from him. Most significantly, I was inspired by how much he believed in his products and how truly innovative he was. Apple was a smaller player than it is now, and its products were expensive relative to the rest of the market, in part because its technology was so ahead of its time. But Steve forged ahead anyway, trusting that so long as he provided the right tools, people would see the value in his work. Even after Steve left, the company continued to work on projects he started, and I stayed with Apple as long as I did because I believed in his vision for the company. During that next decade, I watched as the company grew from a few hundred to several thousand employees, and it was a thrill to work there as it became one of the most influential companies in our time.

Meanwhile, most of my other siblings made their way to the US, and we began the paperwork to sponsor our mom's immigration. In the interim, we missed her and her cooking so much that she sent us her recipes. We picked up fish sauce at our local markets as she directed, but those bottles never smelled like the fish

VIVA STAR COFFEE

CA PHÊ VỢT
NK

sauce we were used to, and our meals never smelled like home and didn't taste like it either. But we didn't think we had an ingredient problem. We thought we were the problem: *No one can cook the way Mom cooks.*

After years of wrangling and red tape, my mom finally joined us in 1990, ferrying with her a small handwritten book of recipes she eventually passed down to us. Her cooking remained delicious, but dishes like thịt kho just didn't have the same fragrance as they once did in Việt Nam. That's when we finally figured it out: The fish sauce here just wasn't the same as the fish sauce there. The version in the States was one-dimensional and smacked of a harsh saltiness. We flipped to the ingredient list and saw fish extract, salt, sugar, other additives and preservatives. That explained it. It didn't taste like the fish sauce we grew up with because it *wasn't* the fish sauce we grew up with. The fish sauce that we knew had fish and salt—that's it.

Nonetheless, being the great cook she was, my mom adapted her recipes to use the fish sauce that was available and figured out that even non-Vietnamese dishes like pasta sauce could be boosted with a drizzle of fish sauce. It was more than good enough for us at the time, though we still reminisced about the old fish sauce. If only, we said, we could get our hands on it stateside.

THE BARREL HOUSE

In the late 1990s and early 2000s, the Internet and tech boom started to really take off worldwide. In 1997, I left Apple to seek new challenges. And I got some new challenges indeed—just not at all where I expected to find them.

I was consulting as a solutions architect, working with Verizon and other telecom and electronics companies. My work took me all over Southeast Asia and, whenever I had some down time, I visited Sài Gòn. I heard Phú Quốc's fish sauce producers were still making amazing fish sauce, so I toured a few local factories on the island. I was able to taste samples of nước mắm drained from the barrel, before it was blended with other ingredients. This first, pure extraction, is so significant that it has a name: nước mắm nhỉ. And *wow*. This was a flavor I had not tasted in over twenty years. It brought me back to being a kid in my mom's kitchen, and the aroma of her thịt kho wafting from the stove. I got enough nước mắm nhỉ to fill a bottle, stowed it in my luggage, and took it home to my mom. She took one whiff and cried.

I went back to Sài Gòn several more times, each time looking to buy retail bottles of nước mắm nhỉ, similar to what I tasted in Phú Quốc. I came up empty. At the time, most fish sauces available outside of Phú Quốc were industrialized, with the fish sauce made in large volumes to sell at low prices. Often the same batch of anchovies went through multiple rounds of extraction, with the

extracted liquid blended with sugars and other additives to compensate for the loss of flavor and color. That industrialized fish sauce was what I saw on American shelves, too. A producer might make a limited bottling of that first extraction, but those bottles of nước mắm nhỉ were too precious to sell. Instead, they were gifted to family or friends.

In 2006, I met the owners of a fish sauce factory in Phú Quốc who wanted to stabilize and expand their business. I struck a deal: I'd invest in their factory if they would repay me in jugs of nước mắm nhỉ. As long as I had enough to keep our family pantry stocked and my mother happy, I'd be happy, too. When I returned from Việt Nam and told my daughters, Tracy and Tiffany, that I bought into a fish sauce company, they thought I was having my own version of a mid-life crisis!

I thought I made a fine investment . . . until about six months later, when the owners abruptly decided they wanted to get out of the fish sauce business altogether. Suddenly, I found myself with the keys to a sixteen-barrel fish sauce facility. And no idea how to make fish sauce.

As it turns out, it is pretty easy to make fish sauce once you have all the suppliers and equipment in place. You get the fish from some fishermen or suppliers, you salt it if it already hasn't been salted, then you pile it into big ten-foot barrels and ferment it. But making *good* fish sauce, the kind that would bring a Vietnamese mother to tears? That's another story.

FORTY DEGREES OF NITROGEN: THE RED BOAT PROCESS

The quality of the fish sauce we made during our first few years of production was incredibly hit or miss. Some barrels produced great fish sauce; others not as much. I was advised to salvage the bad batches with sugar and additives, but that's not what I wanted to do. Rather, I wanted to make pure fish sauce with only anchovies and salt. It had been done before. Why not now?

Fish sauce can be made with a variety of fish, but the black anchovies in the waters of Phú Quốc are exceptionally flavorful when properly fermented. To realize their flavor potential, the anchovies have to be salted with the right type of salt, in precisely the right ratio of salt to fish, immediately after they're pulled out of the water, or else they'll lose their freshness and risk spoilage. The anchovies then need a very expensive ingredient to fully develop their flavor: time.

That was the centuries-old way of making fish sauce. Fish sauce has been a central part of Vietnamese cuisine for hundreds of years; history abounds with stories about fish sauce being gifted to kings and offered as tribute to other rulers. Fish sauce producers during some dynastic eras were required to give a portion of their production to the government. Phú Quốc in particular has long been known for its fish sauce, with generations of master fish-sauce makers who possessed and passed on hard-won knowledge about the meticulous process of fermentation. In fact, Phú Quốc's fish sauce was so highly regarded that the island's producers had to protect their stock from theft using the then-equivalent of a Brink's armored security truck! As Erica J. Peters writes in *Appetites and Aspirations in Vietnam: Food and Drink in the Long Nineteenth Century*, the producers would ship their precious liquid "on specially guarded vessels to favored customers on the mainland."

What makes Phú Quốc's fish sauce so special is the combination of three crucial factors: the umami-rich wild black anchovies in its waters, the process of salting the fish, and the humid climate especially conducive to fermentation.

As I explored the ins and outs of the business, I realized the reason that, despite the island's rich history and fertile environment, precious few producers made fish sauce with only salt and anchovies, and especially not for an overseas market: Past trade embargoes, the industrialization of the fish sauce industry, and byzantine import/export laws had made this old way of making fish sauce simply too expensive and too time-consuming.

I was determined to figure out a way to make the fish sauce of my childhood. But if I wanted to make fish sauce with just salt and anchovies, I needed to control the process from the very beginning, making sure the fish were salted immediately after the catch, with just the right amount of salt. I started

measuring the fish sauce for nitrogen: The higher the nitrogen level, the more protein, the higher the umami, and the deeper the flavor. The higher nitrogen level, then, is a marker of quality. I wanted to make the highest quality of fish sauce I could make using proper fermentation techniques and only the first press of the sauce.

It took three long years and many frustratingly bad batches of fish sauce until we produced a fish sauce with a deep amber glow, smelling of the sea, and redolent with umami. The nitrogen level clocked in at 40 degrees per liter, the highest on the US market at the time and by a large margin at that—most fish sauces on the market measure around 20 degrees of nitrogen. That number also was significant because of what it represents: Fish sauce that measures 40 degrees of nitrogen (or above) could only come from Phú Quốc. No other region in the world has the island's unique climate and access to black anchovies. Combine that with careful salting and fermentation techniques, and you have fish sauce that has no parallel.

When our most important taster, my mother, tried it and gave it her thumbs up, I knew I had it. A great fish sauce made with just wild-caught black anchovies, salt, and time? I had finally cracked the code.

25,000 MILES AND GALLONS OF FISH SAUCE

After investing a substantial amount of time untangling the complex laws and regulations governing food imports, I hauled in those first great batches of fish sauce, decanted them into big jugs, slapped a label with my name and 40°N on it. (I figured those familiar with fish sauce would know immediately what that meant. Those who didn't, I hoped, would give me a chance to start a conversation about fish sauce.) I packed them all into my SUV and drove up and down California, visiting supermarkets and distributors, logging some 25,000 miles of driving that first year. Nam Hoa, a small market in Little Saigon in Orange County, was one of the first markets to stock my fish sauce. The proprietors, Mai Hà and Mai Hoàng, were of the generation who could discern nước mắm nhỉ from the imposters—they knew exactly what I had. I left boxes there on

consignment. I just knew the fish sauce would find a home with others in Little Saigon who missed nước mắm nhỉ.

But Nam Hoa was far and away the exception. The vast majority of markets and retailers I approached flat out rejected the fish sauce without even tasting it. The issue, according to purchasing managers and distributors, was my price point. There was no way they could convince consumers to buy fish sauce at $7, they said, when every other bottle on the shelf was $3 or less. One distributor kindly but bluntly suggested I get out of the business altogether.

That first year was difficult. Sales were incredibly slow, and I was losing heart. Maybe there *was* a reason why no one made fish sauce this way. On top of everything else, I still had my day job working full-time with Verizon.

What kept me going was the encouragement I received, especially from my family. My mother spread the word about the fish sauce to her friends. Ann, my wife, supported my fish sauce obsession from the very beginning, helping me with everything from order fulfillment to shipping. A relative in southern California was a mentor, joining me as I went door to door in Orange County, fish sauce in tow.

Customer feedback also was thrilling. Older Vietnamese folks bought my fish sauce by the caseload, dragging heavy boxes to their cars because they weren't sure if they'd ever see it again. I even received notes from Americans whose first taste of fish sauce was during the war when they were stationed in Phú Quốc; they too were nostalgic for nước mắm nhỉ and ecstatic to find a stateside source.

I also fell back on something I learned from my days at Apple: belief in the product. Steve was convinced that if he provided the platform, people would find him and be empowered to create things from it, even if his products were more expensive

than other companies. Similarly, I knew I couldn't compete in the market in terms of price, but I *knew* I could best it in terms of quality. I knew once cooks learned about my fish sauce, they, like my mom, would find that it had an irreplaceable flavor that boosted many dishes, no matter the cuisine.

After that initial brutal year, I took a step back to reevaluate. Following the advice of a mentor, I rebranded. Because the most important part of the entire fish sauce making process—salting the anchovies—happens on the boat, I decided our brand name and logo should reflect that as well. Thus, Red Boat and our logo: a twin-sailed fishing boat. The boat also has a very personal symbolic meaning to me: The moment I became an adult was the moment I left Việt Nam, and my family, on that fishing boat. We relaunched our fish sauce under the Red Boat label during Tết (Lunar New Year) in early 2011.

At that point, most of our sales came from direct orders on our website. My phone pinged every time we had an order; if I got five pings a day, I was happy. Late in the evening on July 12th—I'll always remember the date—my phone pinged. Then it pinged again. And again. And again. I thought something was wrong with my phone. My phone was fine. Florence Fabricant at the *New York Times* had gotten her hands on a bottle of Red Boat, and her brief post about our fish sauce had just gone live. The next day, the story ran in print. And just like that, I was flooded with orders.

With the help of my family, we converted our living room into a fulfillment center just to handle the volume of orders we received from that one article. It took us at least a week and careful navigation of a mountain of post office boxes to pack and ship out those orders.

That was the turning point. Soon the *Los Angeles Times* mentioned us. *Saveur* put us on their year-end "Saveur 100" list. Ruth Reichl mentioned she liked Red Boat, and we caught the attention of food writers like Andrea Nguyen. Le Bernardin connected with us, and that was the beginning of our relationship with the chef community. And we found an unexpected home in the Whole30 and paleo communities, who discovered our fish sauce as a great way to add flavor without sugar or additives. Those years of frustration, stress, and self-doubt were starting to pay off.

In late 2011, my mother fell ill, and I quit my job with Verizon to care for her. During those last few months, I reflected on how much she had shepherded me through so much, from preparing me for my journey out of Việt Nam to cheering me on through all my frustrations with making fish sauce. She passed in March 2012, happy to see me succeed in my quest.

Red Boat today is the legacy of my relationship with my mom. I started this journey because I wanted to make her happy. And Red Boat's fish sauce, I think, did just that.

RED BOAT TODAY: A PHAMILY BUSINESS

Today, I'm proud to say Red Boat has become a true "Phamily" business. My daughter Tracy manages sales and finance. My son, Kevin, is the production supervisor, and my youngest, Tiffany, handles marketing and food safety compliance.

A lot has changed since Red Boat officially launched in 2011. Our barrel house has grown from 16 barrels to 190, each capable of holding up to 14 tons of salted anchovies. In addition to our signature 40°N Red Boat Fish Sauce, we also occasionally bottle fish sauce that measures a stunning 50°N. As I spent more time in Phú Quốc, I became obsessed with the island's famed aromatic peppercorns as well as delicious palm sugar from Cambodia. We now work with local farmers to bring both to the US.

What hasn't changed is our amazing community of Red Boat Fish Sauce fans. Many of our fans have been seeking us out since those early days when I carted around my fish sauce in unwieldy jugs. We are so, so fortunate to have garnered such a loyal following of fish sauce aficionados.

OUR PHAMILY RECIPES

In writing this cookbook, we pulled together recipes from a few different sources. First and foremost, my mother. We adapted and updated a number of her recipes—the same recipes in the notebook she brought with her when she immigrated to the US—including a few of my favorites growing up, like her cháo bồi and thịt ba rọi cuốn (pork roast). We also included favorite dishes from my own family table, plus new favorites that we've developed at Red Boat over the years. And, finally, a few of our chef friends generously contributed a few recipes, too.

Taken together, the recipes in this book reflect the myriad of ways Red Boat Fish Sauce can be used. They also reflect its versatility: We'll show you how we use fish sauce from breakfast to dinner, and in Vietnamese and non-Vietnamese dishes alike. The vast majority of our recipes use fish sauce in one way or another, but we also have a handful of recipes that showcase our palm sugar. It makes such a big difference in dishes like kho and in certain desserts that it's worth saving a spot for it in your pantry, too.

As you cook through the book, you'll notice a mix of quick dishes that take less than an hour to get to the table, others that are weekend projects, and still others that could benefit from many hands pitching in to wrap or roll. If you need assistance on selecting what to make and when, flip to the back of the book and use our Menu Planning suggestions.

Throughout these pages we'll take you on a few side trips: to evaporation ponds where salt is harvested; to our barrel house in Phú Quốc where the freshly caught anchovies ferment for over a year; and to the buzzing streets of Sài Gòn where I grew up.

Whether you grew up with fish sauce like I did or you're a fish sauce novice, we hope our cookbook will inspire you to find new ways to incorporate our fish sauce into your everyday cooking.

It's been a decade since Red Boat officially launched in 2011, meaning this cookbook comes just as we're celebrating our ten-year anniversary. On behalf of myself and everyone at Red Boat, thank you for making room in your pantry for us over the last ten years. We can't think of a better way to celebrate this milestone anniversary than to share our family recipes with you.

PHAMILY PANTRY FAVORITES

The majority of the ingredients you need to make the dishes in this book can be found at your local Asian or Southeast Asian markets, or at large supermarket chains. This isn't an exhaustive list of everything we use in the book; rather, we hope these notes on sourcing, selecting, preparing, and storing our favorite ingredients will help you as you cook through our recipes.

BÁNH TRÁNG (RICE PAPER WRAPPERS)

Dried rice paper in rounds or squares are used to make wraps and egg rolls. For fresh rolls, bánh tráng made with both rice and tapioca will be especially pliable so you can more easily fold it over your fillings. For fried rolls, bánh tráng with only rice, salt, and water will result in a better fry. Out of the package, the dried rice paper is brittle. To use, dip it in warm water for just a few seconds to rehydrate, then lay it flat on your plate. Pile on the fillings, then roll.

BEAN SPROUTS

Use mung bean sprouts, the most common bean sprout you'll find at most markets. Look for sprouts that are bright and firm; avoid limp or dry sprouts. Store them in the fridge in a container of water and change the water every other day.

BUTTER

We use unsalted butter in all our recipes.

COCONUT MILK AND COCONUT CREAM

Coconut milk is extracted from the flesh of mature coconuts and blended with water. Coconut cream has less water content and is thicker and richer. We use the unsweetened version of both in our recipes. The brand Kara makes excellent coconut milk and cream packaged in cans and boxes.

COCONUT WATER AND COCONUT SODA

Coconut water extracted from fresh coconuts is superior than anything canned, boxed, or bottled (see page 59 for tips on how to crack open a coconut). Otherwise, look for pure coconut water without additives or flavorings. A few of our recipes use coconut soda, which is carbonated water with some sugar and coconut extract. The most common brand is Coco Rico. If you don't have coconut soda, you can substitute an equal amount of coconut water plus sugar to taste.

CHILES

Fiery Thai chiles (or bird's-eye chile) are a must-have; though, in a pinch, green, slender serrano chiles will do. The spice level for chiles varies widely depending on the source and season. To reduce the heat, remove the seed, pith, and ribs before cooking or eating.

DRIED WOOD EAR MUSHROOMS

Sometimes labeled "black fungus," wood ear mushrooms provide texture to a variety of dishes. To rehydrate, submerge them in warm water for about ten minutes, then drain and rinse to remove any remaining grit.

EGGS

We use large eggs in all our recipes.

RED BOAT FISH SAUCE

Of course! Our fish sauce is made with just two ingredients: wild-caught black anchovies and salt. The original, and the most popular, of our fish sauce line is our 40°N Fish Sauce (the 40°N refers to the nitrogen level per liter of fish sauce; the higher the nitrogen level, the higher the protein content and the more pronounced the umami). That's the version we use for all the cooking in this book.

We also offer a few special editions of our fish sauce, including a 50°N Phamily Reserve and the 50°N fish sauce aged in hardwood smoked and maple bourbon barrels. Those are best reserved for dipping and special occasions. And, finally, we also occasionally offer Red Boat Mắm Nêm, which is an unfiltered version of our fish sauce. With the particulates left in the bottle rather than sieved out, the mắm nêm is markedly brinier than filtered fish sauce.

We recommend using your bottle of Red Boat within a year.

GINGER

Ginger at Asian and specialty markets tends to come in rhizomes that are fresher and larger than what you find in large supermarket chains. Except for instances when a whole piece of ginger is used, we offer specific volume measurements rather than segment sizes in our recipes. When shopping, look for ginger that's heavy for its size. In addition, examine its skin: A shriveled skin indicates the ginger is past its prime and likely has dried out. Instead, select a firm piece with taut skin.

HERBS

Many Vietnamese meals are accompanied by a platter of herbs for curating every bite to your taste. In most recipes, we note the herbs to serve with the dish, but you can always make your own herb platter by selecting some or all of the following herbs and piling them on a plate along with assorted green lettuces. The herbs will last longer if you protect them from cold temperatures; if you have a very small cooler, place the herbs there, and then stow the entire cooler in the fridge. Otherwise, place the herbs in a paper bag set inside another paper bag and tuck it into your fridge's crisper drawer. Wash the herbs right before you use them.

CILANTRO: Unless otherwise specified, use the entire cilantro: the leaves, stems, and roots.

MINT: Mint lends freshness to many Vietnamese dishes. You can also use spearmint.

THAI BASIL: The Vietnamese name for this herb is húng quế, which

FIRST PRESS – 100% PURE

RED
BOAT
FISH SAUCE

40°N

MADE IN
Phú Quốc Island
VIETNAM
NET 17 FL OZ (500 mL)

RED
BOAT
FISH SAUCE
40°N

FIRST PRESS – 100% PURE
RED
BOAT
FISH SAUCE
40°N
MADE IN
Phú Quốc Island
VIETNAM
NET 8.45 FL OZ (250 mL)

means cinnamon basil. That name captures its flavor perfectly.

RAU RĂM: Also known as Vietnamese coriander, rau răm has long pointed leaves, very often with a blush of purple in the center. It's aromatic, grassy, and warming, almost always used raw or as a final garnish.

SAWTOOTH HERB: This herb with narrow, serrated leaves can be found at Southeast Asian and Latin American markets. Look for it under the names ngò gai and culantro, respectively. Its flavor is more intense and concentrated than cilantro.

TÍA TÔ (VIETNAMESE PERILLA): Tía tô is a large-leafed purple herb with aromatic, spicy, earthy notes. It is similar to shiso, but more robust and assertive.

HOT SAUCE

For extra heat, our favorites are Huy Fong's Sriracha and Cholula Hot Sauce. Stock your pantry with your favorite.

LẠP XƯỞNG (CHINESE SAUSAGE)

Also called lap cheong or Chinese sausage, these cured sausages are made with pork and pork fat, although some brands may add other ground meats. We prefer the lạp xưởng from California Sausage Inc.

LEMONGRASS

Lemongrass's flavor resides primarily in the oils in the root end of the stalk. For that reason, look for juicy, plump stalks, or stalks that seem heavy for their size. Frozen minced lemongrass found in Asian markets will be better than lemongrass that is dried out and brittle.

To mince, remove the dry outer layers and wash off any residual dirt. Chop off and discard about ¼ inch of the lemongrass base. With a very sharp knife, thinly slice the lemongrass into coins—the thinner the better. Continue slicing until halfway up the lemongrass stalk, then discard the remaining top. Chop the lemongrass coins into a fine mince. It's ready for use.

MAGGI SEASONING

A little bit of this intensely flavorful vegetable-based seasoning goes a long way—usually, just a few drops in a bánh mì or in marinades and sauces are all you need.

MAKRUT LIMES

The aromatic double-lobed leaves from knobby makrut limes are used to flavor soups, stews, and salads. The limes are often zested as well, but the juice itself is astringent and less often used.

MẮM TÔM

This thick, intensely brackish sauce is made from fermented shrimp and is full of complex savory and sweet notes. You can find mắm tôm at Asian markets; a little bit will go a long way, so a small jar will last quite a while in your fridge. We prefer Indonesian or Thai brands.

NOODLES

We have a variety of noodles in our pantry.

BÚN (RICE VERMICELLI): Used in rice noodle salads and wraps, bún is packaged in bundles and often labeled as "rice sticks." Bún needs to be cooked before using; to do so, boil the noodles for just a few minutes, then rinse. Because boiling and rinsing the noodles remove

much of their starch, these tend to be lighter than the pre-cooked dry noodles used in phở. Depending on the brand, the length of the noodles can be quite long; we like the brands labeled "giang tây," which are cut into smaller 8-inch strands.

CELLOPHANE NOODLES: Used in soups and as part of the filling for egg rolls and other dishes, these noodles are also known as glass noodles, bean thread noodles, miến, bún tàu, and, somewhat confusingly, vermicelli. To make sure you're picking up the noodles you need, look at the ingredients: Cellophane noodles should be made with mung beans.

BÁNH PHỞ (PHỞ NOODLES): Bánh phở are flat rice noodles specifically for use in phở. Dried phở noodles are par-cooked, if not fully cooked, so they just need a very brief dunk in hot water to soften. Bánh phở tươi, or fresh phở noodles, can be found at Vietnamese markets, bakeries, and delis.

ITALIAN PASTA: We always have a few boxes of wheat-based dried Italian pasta in our cupboard to make dishes like spaghetti at home. We are fans of the organic dried pasta from Semolina Artisanal Pasta, available at many specialty grocers and online.

OILS

We have a few types of oil in our pantry. For all oils, buy the best quality you can afford. Oil also does go rancid, so either select what you will use within a few months or replace your bottle after six months.

EXTRA-VIRGIN OLIVE OIL: We always have a good quality extra virgin olive oil on our countertop.

NEUTRAL OIL: These are oils that have a neutral flavor and a high smoke point, which make them ideal for frying. Vegetable, canola, and grapeseed are all neutral oils.

SESAME OIL: Look for pure sesame oil rather than sesame oil that has been blended with other oils. Pure sesame oil is more expensive, but since it's used in small quantities in most recipes, it will last a few months. That said, even a drop of rancid sesame oil will ruin a dish, so keep an eye on the oil and replace it if it has degraded.

RED BOAT PALM SUGAR

We source our palm sugar from family-owned farms in Cambodia. Made with the sap from palmyra trees, our palm sugar is rich and nutty, with an undertone of caramel. We love to use it in kho (caramelized braises) and in desserts. If you don't have palm sugar, use an equal amount of granulated sugar. See page 251 for more about how we source and use our palm sugar.

RICE

To accompany our everyday meals, we use jasmine rice, a long-grain variety, and we especially like the Three Ladies brand. Certain dishes, like cơm tấm (seared pork chops with rice), are often served with broken rice, which are grains of rice that have been fractured during the milling process. Bags of broken rice can be found at Asian grocers; alternatively, substitute it with whole-grain jasmine rice. For sticky rice dishes and desserts, we use a short-grain sweet rice (sometimes labeled "glutinous rice"), and we especially recommend Koda Farms Sho-Chiku-Bai Sweet Rice.

RICE FLOURS

There are two kinds of rice flour. The first is made from finely milling long-grain rice. The second is sweet rice flour, sometimes labeled as glutinous, made from finely milling sweet rice. For sweet rice flour, we like Koda Farms' Blue Star Mochiko Sweet Rice Flour.

RICE POWDER

Rice powder is often tossed into dishes for fragrance and flavor, and it can also be used as a binding agent. Toasting the powder brings out a lovely nuttiness, which we prefer, and toasted rice powder can be found at Asian markets (sometimes labeled as "roasted" rice powder). But if you have sweet rice in your pantry, you can easily make as much or as little toasted rice powder as you need: Place a few handfuls of sweet rice in a dry skillet over medium heat. Toast the rice for fifteen to thirty minutes, depending on how much you have, stirring the kernels constantly so they don't burn and toast evenly. Once they're pale brown in color, transfer the rice to a baking sheet to cool completely, then grind to a powder. Store the toasted rice powder in an airtight container for up to three months.

SHALLOTS

Like ginger, shallots vary widely in size. For that reason, most of our recipes indicate the

volume amount, rather than how many bulbs to use. We also always have fried shallots on hand to use as a garnish. You can use store-bought fried shallots, but frying your own (see page 290) is not difficult and significantly tastier and crisper than any packaged version. When buying shallots for frying, select the largest shallots you can find to make the peeling and chopping process less laborious.

SOY SAUCE

We use Kikkoman and San-J for our soy sauce.

SALTS

RED BOAT SALT:

After we drain the fish sauce from our fermentation barrels, we harvest the salt that remains behind. That salt, infused with the flavor of the anchovies, is delicious. Unless otherwise noted, you can substitute Red Boat Salt for kosher salt in the recipes in this book. If you want to experiment with substituting kosher salt for Red Boat Salt, start with half the amount stated in the recipe and adjust to taste.

KOSHER SALT: We keep Morton's kosher salt on hand. Unless otherwise specified, you can substitute kosher salt for Red Boat Salt in our recipes and adjust to taste.

SPICES

We recommend buying whole spices where you can, and only buying enough to last six to twelve months. We also suggest investing in a small grinder so you can grind the spices only when needed. Once ground, the spices will start to lose their brightness and potency. These are the spices we keep stocked:

ANNATTO SEEDS: These seeds are as red-orange as a barrel in our barrel house. When the seeds are simmered in oil, they release their color, and the scarlet-hued oil is then used to color and subtly flavor dishes. You can make a batch of annatto oil (see page 287) and store it in your fridge for up to two months. There is no substitute for annatto oil; for our recipes, you can safely omit it if you don't have any on hand. If you do leave it out, just note you'll lose a bit of color in the final dish.

CINNAMON: Whatever type of cinnamon you prefer, pick up cinnamon sticks rather than ground cinnamon. Cinnamon sticks last much longer than ground cinnamon and are just as widely available. Grind it fresh using a fine grater like a Microplane.

STAR ANISE: This star-shaped spice is licorice in flavor and is a must for a variety of dishes like phở. It's usually tossed in whole during the cooking process, then removed before serving.

TURMERIC: We love the turmeric from Diaspora Co.

PEPPERCORNS

RED BOAT PHÚ QUỐC PEPPERCORNS: In addition to fish sauce, Phú Quốc is well known for its fragrant peppercorns. We work directly with a Phú Quốc farm to bring this special spice to the US; we don't always have it in stock, but when we do, we put it in our pepper mill and use it whenever we need freshly ground black pepper.

WHITE PEPPERCORNS: White peppercorns are more tingly than black peppercorns. In some cases, they're used for aesthetic reasons. For our recipes, you can use black peppercorns if you don't have any white peppercorns on hand.

TAMARIND PASTE

Made of pods of the tamarind tree, tamarind paste is jammy, with a bright acidity and a distinct note of sourness. You can find dried blocks of tamarind paste at Asian, South Asian, Southeast Asian, and Latin American markets, and many major supermarket chains carry it as well. Rehydrate the paste in warm water and strain before using.

TAPIOCA STARCH

Tapioca starch (or flour) is made from cassava and is used for coating meats and thickening sauces.

VINEGARS

We keep distilled white vinegar, apple cider vinegar, champagne vinegar, and rice vinegar all on hand for cooking, pickling, and making salad dressings.

CHAPTER 1

BREAK FAST

RED BOAT-CURED BACON

This recipe for bacon is a riff on the one served at Good Girl Dinette, the restaurant that Diep Tran ran before she joined Red Boat as our R&D chef. To make the bacon, start with an entire slab of pork belly and coat it in a rub made with Red Boat Salt or Fish Sauce, coriander, cinnamon, and other warming spices (as with most spices, the fresher, the better—so grind them fresh if you can). The rub cures the belly beautifully and, after a four-day cure, the belly is ready to be roasted into bacon. Any leftovers will freeze easily. If you don't feel like taking on a four-day project, Diep also has a faster version using store-bought strips (see page 30). Whichever version you make, you'll understand why this bacon was a star of Good Girl Dinette's weekend brunch.

MAKES 5 POUNDS

¼ cup ground black pepper
1 tablespoon ground star anise
2 tablespoons ground cinnamon
½ cup ground coriander
2½ tablespoons Red Boat Salt or **½** cup Red Boat Fish Sauce
⅓ pound (⅔ cup) packed brown sugar
⅔ cup minced garlic
5 pounds center-cut pork belly, skin removed
½ cup applewood chips

Make the spice rub and cure the pork

1. To make the spice rub, begin in a dry skillet by toasting the black pepper, star anise, cinnamon, and coriander over medium heat until fragrant,1 to 2 minutes, being sure to shake the pan constantly so the spices don't burn. Transfer the spices to a mixing bowl.
2. Add the salt or fish sauce, brown sugar, and garlic to the spices. Stir to combine.
3. Trim the pork belly into 7 x 11-inch slabs. To make it easier to slice the belly into bacon slices, take care to trim the pork so its grain is perpendicular to the longer side of each slab. Massage the spice rub into the slabs and place them in resealable food bags. Refrigerate the pork for 4 days, flipping the bags on the second day to ensure that spice rub evenly coats the pork belly.

Make the bacon

4. On the fourth day, place the applewood chips in a bowl and cover with water. Soak the chips for at least 1 hour, then drain. Cut two pieces of aluminum foil into 8 x 8-inch pieces and layer them on top of each other. Place the soaked chips in the center of the double-stacked aluminum foil, then fold up the sides and crimp to create a closed pouch. Use a paring knife to perforate the top of the pouch to allow smoke to vent, then place the pouch in the center of the oven floor. Heat the oven to 225°F. This is essentially a makeshift smoker, so the chips will start to smoke.
5. Remove the pork from the bags and place it on a wire rack on a baking sheet. Place the baking sheet in the center of the oven and roast the pork until its internal temperature is 140°F, about 2 hours. Turn the oven off and keep the pork belly in the oven for another 30 minutes.
6. Remove the pork belly from the oven. When the belly has cooled completely, slice each slab into ¼-inch-thick slices.
7. To crisp the bacon using your oven, increase the temperature to 400°F. Set a wire rack onto a baking sheet and lay the bacon strips in a single layer on the rack. When the oven comes to temperature, place the baking sheet in the center of the oven and bake for 15 to 20 minutes, rotating the pan after 10 minutes to ensure the slices crisp evenly.

   Alternatively, you can crisp the bacon on the stove. Place the strips in a cold heavy-bottomed frying pan. Cook on low heat, flipping the strips every 2 minutes, until the bacon is crisp.

This recipe yields quite a bit of bacon. If you aren't eating right away, you can slice the bacon, bundle it in 1-pound parcels, and store them in the freezer for up to six months. To do so, lay the bacon slices onto a large piece of parchment paper, shingling the slices so they'll lay flat. Fold up the parchment to cover the slices, then wrap everything up in plastic wrap. Store the bacon in the freezer until ready to use.

QUICK RED BOAT BACON

This spice mix is enough for 1 pound of store-bought bacon. You also can double or triple the mix and store it in a jar, covered, in your spice cabinet for future use.

MAKES 1 POUND

½ tablespoon ground black pepper
½ teaspoon ground star anise
1¼ teaspoons ground cinnamon
1⅔ tablespoons ground coriander
1½ teaspoons Red Boat Salt or **1½** tablespoons Red Boat Fish Sauce
½ cup brown sugar
1 pound sliced bacon

1. In a dry skillet over medium heat, toast the black pepper, star anise, cinnamon, and coriander until fragrant, 1 to 2 minutes, shaking the pan constantly so the spices don't burn. Transfer the spices to a mixing bowl.
2. Add the salt or fish sauce and brown sugar to the spices. Stir to combine.
3. Massage the spice rub onto the bacon, being sure to evenly coat both sides of each strip. Marinate for at least 10 minutes.
4. To crisp the bacon using your oven, set the temperature to 400°F. Set a wire rack on a baking sheet and lay the bacon strips in a single layer on the rack. When the oven comes to temperature, place the pan in the center of the oven and bake for 15 to 20 minutes, rotating the pan after 10 minutes to ensure the slices crisp evenly.

   Alternatively, you can crisp the bacon on the stove. Place the strips in a cold heavy-bottomed frying pan. Cook over low heat, flipping the strips every 2 minutes, until the bacon is crisp.

BACON AND EGG BREAKFAST BÁNH MÌ

One of our favorite ways of using fish sauce is also one of the simplest: adding it to eggs. While eggs scrambled with fish sauce and served with toast makes for an excellent breakfast, we take things one step further and turn the eggs into a filling for a delicious breakfast sandwich. In addition to the fluffy scrambled eggs, the sandwich is loaded with bacon and the hallmark components of a good bánh mì: an umami-laden spread, crunchy pickles, and cilantro.

The pickle is a quick one made with red onion, but if you already have a jar of pickled daikon and carrots or another pickle in your fridge, feel free to use that instead. As for the bread itself, a crusty Vietnamese-style baguette is classic of course, but you also can use ciabatta or a bolillo roll. Brew up a steaming hot cup of coffee, and you'll have yourself a perfect leisurely weekend breakfast.

MAKES 1 BÁNH MÌ

¼ cup sliced red onion
2 tablespoons white vinegar
1 cup ice water
2 eggs
½ teaspoon Red Boat Fish Sauce
1 pinch ground black pepper
1 teaspoon canola, grapeseed, vegetable, or other neutral oil
1 (6- to 8-inch) baguette
chicken liver pâté (optional)
2 strips Red Boat–Cured Bacon (page 28), or store-bought bacon, fully cooked
Handful cilantro leaves
Cilantro Mayonnaise (page 284), or Kewpie Mayonnaise

→ *continued*

BEURRE
BRETEL
BUTTER

1. Place the sliced onions, vinegar, and ice water in a mixing bowl. Soak the onions for 10 minutes, then drain and set aside.
2. Combine the eggs, fish sauce, and black pepper in a mixing bowl. Beat to blend.
3. In a hot pan over medium-high heat, pour the oil. Add the eggs to the pan. When the edges of the eggs start to set, push the edges toward the center of the pan. Continue pushing the eggs to the center of the pan until the eggs are just set, about 1½ minutes. Transfer the scrambled eggs to a plate.
4. To assemble the bánh mì, toast the baguette whole in your oven or toaster oven until crisp. Split the baguette in half and spread the bottom half with a generous layer of chicken liver pâté, if using. Place the scrambled eggs on the bottom half, then the bacon, a few of the quick-pickled onions, and a handful of cilantro leaves. Spread the mayonnaise on the top half of the baguette and serve.

BUILD YOUR OWN BÁNH MÌ

Bread

An airy bánh mì is classic, but you can use other types of breads with soft crumbs and thin crusts, too. Ciabattas, bolillos, and telera rolls all work well.

Spreads

Our Cilantro Mayonnaise (page 284) was made with bánh mì in mind. Alternatively (or in addition!), layer creamy chicken liver pâté onto the sandwich.

Fillings

If you have leftovers from any of the meaty dishes in this book, chances are they'll be terrific stuffed into a bánh mì. In particular, leftovers from the following are ideal next-day sandwich fillings:

- Thịt Ba Rọi Cuốn (Pork Roast) (page 159)
- The pork patties or belly from Bún Chả Hà Nội (page 153)
- The Ultimate Thịt Heo Quay (Crispy Pork Belly) (page 156)
- Red Boat Ginger-Cilantro Fried Chicken (page 189)
- Mom's Gà Quay (Roast Chicken) (page 193)
- Red Boat Holiday Turkey with Gravy (page 239)
- Chạo Tôm (Sugarcane Shrimp) (page 116)
- Nem Nướng (Grilled Pork Meatballs) (page 149)

Pickles

For a bit of acid, pickled daikon and carrots (page 264) are common in bánh mì.

You also can experiment with different pickles, especially if you already have some stashed in your fridge.

For example, make your own BLT with our bacon (page 28) and pickled green tomatoes using the same method outlined in our recipe for Pickled Cabbage (page 264).

Garnishes

The final touch to a great bánh mì: a few bright sprigs of cilantro and, optionally, sliced jalapeño or serrano chiles, plus a sprinkle of fried shallots (page 290).

MIẾN GÀ (CHICKEN SOUP WITH CELLOPHANE NOODLES)

We have noodle soups for breakfast very often, and one of our favorites is miến gà, chicken soup with cellophane (sometimes called glass) noodles, seasoned with some fish sauce, and garnished with cilantro. The most complex part is making the stock, as it takes a little bit of time—to save time in the morning, you can make the stock the evening before. Alternatively, if you already made our Chicken Stock (page 292) and have some chicken on hand, just poach the meat in the stock in the morning, shred it, and drop it into your bowl along with the noodles and garnishes. In addition to a great way to start your day, the soup is so nourishing that it doubles as warm comfort on any sick day. The fat in the legs is packed with flavor, but if you prefer a leaner stock, skim the fat off the top of the stock before ladling it into bowls.

SERVES 4 TO 6

6 to **9** ounces cellophane noodles
2½ pounds chicken legs
2 teaspoons kosher salt
1 pound white or yellow onions, quartered
2 teaspoons whole black peppercorns or **2** Thai chiles
4 to **6** tablespoons Red Boat Fish Sauce, divided
8 scallions
1 ounce whole ginger
1 cup chopped cilantro
1 cup chopped scallions
1 cup store-bought or homemade Fried Shallots (page 290)

FOR SERVING

Ground black pepper
Lemongrass-Chile Oil (page 288) (optional)

→ *continued*

1. Soak the cellophane noodles in room temperature water. Set aside.
2. Make the stock: Butcher the legs at the joint, separating the thigh from the drumstick. Add the chicken pieces, salt, and 4 quarts of cold water to a stockpot, then place the pot in the refrigerator. Let the chicken soak for at least an hour, or overnight.
3. Drain the water and refill the pot with more cold water. Swish the chicken around in the water to loosen any residual impurities sticking to the surface of the chicken, then drain the water again.
4. Add the quartered onion, black peppercorns or Thai chiles, 2 tablespoons fish sauce, and 2 quarts cold water. Over high heat, bring the pot to a boil. Skim the impurities that rise to the surface.
5. Reduce the heat to a low simmer. If large bubbles break the surface, the flame is too high; lower the heat so the surface of the water just trembles (about 200°F). Simmer the stock for 30 minutes.
6. After 30 minutes, turn off the heat and add the scallion stalks and ginger to the pot. Cover and steep for 30 minutes. Remove the chicken and set aside to cool.
7. Strain the entire broth through a fine-mesh cloth, then return to the stockpot. Add 2 more tablespoons of fish sauce to the stock. Taste and add up to 2 more tablespoons of fish sauce if you feel the stock isn't salty enough. Set the stock aside.
8. Remove and discard the skin and bones from chicken. Shred the meat and set aside.
9. To assemble the soup, bring the chicken stock to a simmer. Separately, bring a medium pot of water to a simmer.
10. For each serving, place a handful of cellophane noodles into a noodle basket and dunk into the simmering water until the noodles turn translucent, 15 to 30 seconds. If you don't have a noodle basket, you can drop the handful of noodles into the water instead, and pull them out with a strainer.
11. Tap the noodle basket against the lip of the pot, to shake the excess water from the noodles, then pour the noodles into a bowl.
12. Add some shredded chicken, cilantro, and chopped scallions to the bowl. Ladle 1½ cups chicken stock over the noodles and top with a handful of fried shallots. Repeat with the rest of the noodles, chicken, cilantro, scallions, and stock. Crack some black pepper over each bowl. Serve hot with the lemongrass-chile oil on the side for guests to add to their bowls as they wish.

MUSHROOM AND EGG CHÁO (PORRIDGE)

A steaming hot bowl of cháo first thing in the morning is a bowl of pure comfort. We make our porridge with jasmine rice, but you can certainly use brown rice instead (just note that it will take a bit more time on the stove for the kernels to break down). For a silkier porridge, you can replace ¼ cup of the rice with sweet rice; if you do so, keep an eye on the pot and stir often, as the sweet rice will have a strong tendency to stick to the bottom of the pot if left undisturbed. The mushrooms that top the porridge—which are coated in fish sauce, ginger, and cilantro, then roasted until sizzling and caramelized—can be made while the cháo simmers, but you can also make it the night before, along with the marinated eggs.

SERVES 4 TO 6

PORRIDGE

1 cup jasmine rice
1 cup minced white onion
2 teaspoons minced ginger
3½ tablespoons Red Boat Fish Sauce, divided
3 cups Pork or Chicken Stock (pages 294 and 292) or store-bought

MUSHROOMS

2 large garlic cloves
½ cup roughly chopped cilantro
1 tablespoon roughly chopped ginger
3 tablespoons grapeseed, canola, vegetable, or other neutral oil
1 teaspoon granulated sugar
½ teaspoon ground black pepper
1 teaspoon ground coriander
1½ teaspoons Red Boat Fish Sauce
1 pound oyster mushrooms

GARNISH

4 to **6** Fish Sauce–Marinated Eggs (page 42), sliced in half
1 cup sliced scallions
1 cup chopped cilantro
White pepper (optional)

Start the porridge

1. In a medium mixing bowl, soak the rice in 1 quart cold water. Swirl the rice around the bowl a few times to loosen the starch. Drain the starchy water, refill the bowl with clean water, and repeat this process three times.
2. Drain the rice one final time. In a heavy-bottomed pot over high heat, combine the rice, onion, ginger, 3 tablespoons of fish sauce, and 6 cups of cold water.
3. Bring the pot to a boil, stirring the rice to break up any clumps. Once the water starts to boil, bring down the heat to very low, cover, and simmer for 1 hour.

Meanwhile, roast the mushrooms

4. Preheat the oven to 400°F.
5. Use a mortar and pestle to pound the garlic, cilantro, and ginger into a paste.
6. Transfer the mixture to a large mixing bowl, then add the oil, sugar, pepper, coriander, and 1½ teaspoons fish sauce. Stir to combine.
7. Slice and discard the woody bottom stems of the oyster mushroom clusters. Separate the clusters into individual mushrooms.
8. Add the mushrooms to the ginger-cilantro marinade and toss to coat. Transfer the mushrooms to a large baking sheet, spreading them in one even layer.
9. Roast the mushrooms until they're caramelized at the edges, 20 to 25 minutes, rotating the baking sheet at the 10-minute mark. Once roasted and cool enough to handle, shred the mushrooms by hand, then set them aside while you finish the porridge.

Finish the porridge

10. After the porridge has simmered for 1 hour, uncover the pot and loosen any rice stuck to the bottom. By this time, the rice should have fully burst and melted into a thick porridge. If you still see intact rice kernels, cover and simmer the porridge for another 10 to 25 minutes.
11. Add the stock to the pot and simmer for another 10 minutes.
12. Taste the porridge and add the remaining ½ tablespoon fish sauce, if desired.
13. For each serving, ladle 1½ to 2 cups of porridge into a bowl. Top with shredded mushrooms, marinated egg, a handful of sliced scallions and cilantro leaves, and a shake of white pepper if using. Serve hot.

MY MOTHER'S RECIPE BOOK

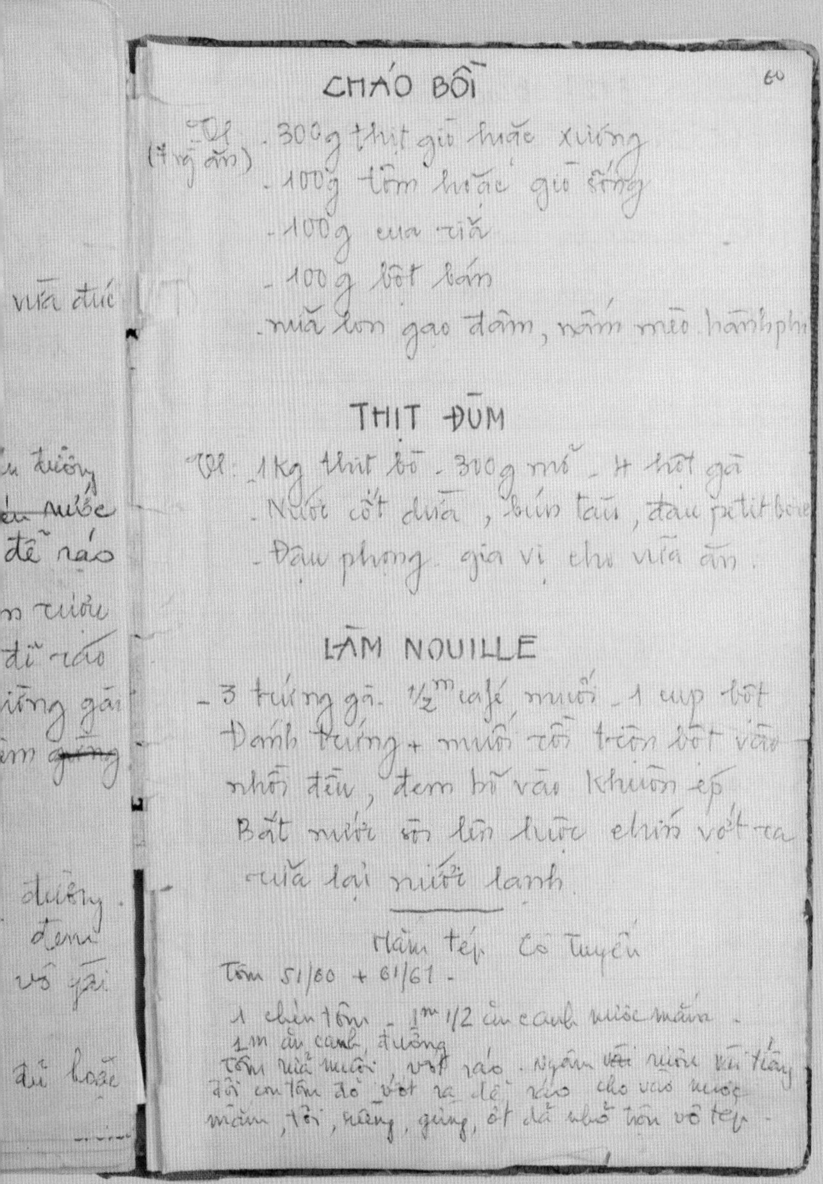

Tucked safely on a shelf in the kitchen of my sister Điệp's house is a small notebook. Some of the binding on the green spine has come loose; the red cover is cracked. Inside, the sixty or so graph-lined pages are filled with neat, cursive handwriting: *Cháo Bồi, Bánh Bao, Thịt Ba Rọi Cuốn*. This was my mother's notebook, filled with her recipes and cooking notes. We consider her book of recipes the foundation for our own book of recipes here.

It's a near miracle that we have her recipe book at all. She actually recorded her recipes in four cherished notebooks. Soon after my siblings and I arrived in the US, we wrote to our mom, homesick, telling her how much we missed her cooking. In response, she sent us two notebooks filled with her recipes—but those notebooks never reached us, and we never did find out where they landed. The third book made it stateside, but it also slipped away from us, lost in one move or another. The fourth notebook was ferried over by my mother herself when she left Việt Nam for the US. When my mom passed, my sister Điệp, who so often was my mom's second pair of hands in the kitchen, held on to it, and it's Điệp who has kept this memento safe ever since.

My mother's four-volume set of recipe books contained different recipes, so there's no way of knowing what gems she squirreled away in her other three books. But the one book we do have reveals a lot about her as a cook. She had formal French culinary training, and her recipes display quite a range of cooking. Her book includes recipes for candies, pastries, sauces, condiments, meat dishes, vegetable platters, and cakes. She was quite a cosmopolitan cook; in addition to Vietnamese dishes, various French braises and stews, numerous dim sum, and Malaysian noodles are represented in her pages.

What my mom didn't write down in her book is just as fascinating as what she did include. For example, in her recipe for bánh pâté chaud, the savory meat pie, she meticulously details the steps required to make puff pastry—an indication that she didn't make it every day. Her recipe for the meat filling, on the other hand, is more spare; about the only thing she jotted down reads like a reminder: the ratio of pork to liver. Our guess is she had a standard filling committed to memory; her addition of pork and liver built on that knowledge and was specific to her pâté chaud. Details like that reveal my mom's culinary style, as that combination of pork and liver recalls country-style pâtés, which is fitting for a pastry with French roots.

Given there are techniques or dishes that she considered so basic or foundational as to not be worth documenting, we had to fill in some gaps as we worked through her notebook. Some gaps were easy to bridge. Even if she didn't explicitly say how to serve her thịt ba rọi cuốn (pork roast), for example, we know it's usually sliced for a platter of cold cuts or intended to stuff a bánh mì.

Other things were much harder to decipher. A few recipes called for ingredients we didn't recognize. For recipes where we didn't have much other than a list of ingredients to work with, we made our best guess about how to prepare, combine, and cook the dish. The final step in many of her recipes is a very open-ended instruction to season "to taste." We relied on our own taste buds and memories to interpret what "to taste" might mean. We also were guided and inspired by the work of the scholar and journalist Toni Tipton-Martin, whose two books, *The Jemima Code: Two Centuries of African American Cookbooks* and *Jubilee: Recipes from Two Centuries of African American Cooking*, are master classes on interpreting and adapting historical recipes.

Over the years, my mom updated her book with new dishes and added new notes to old recipes. My sister Điệp took up the mantle, and she, too, keeps the book updated with her notes and recipes. Both Điệps (my sister and Red Boat's R&D chef, Diep Tran) were instrumental in helping us adapt my mother's recipes. With their help, we think we managed to stay true to the spirit of my mom's cooking. That said, this process is a useful reminder that *all* recipes are dynamic, including the ones we have in this book. We encourage you to adapt and modify our recipes to fit your home kitchen, too.

FISH SAUCE–MARINATED EGGS

Drop some soft-boiled eggs in an umami-sweet marinade of fish sauce and palm sugar, and they'll be ready to eat in just a few hours' time. Slice one in half and top off your bowl of porridge, or have it with toast in the morning. For a quick and easy lunch, try the eggs with a simple bowl of steamed rice or noodles.

MAKES 6 EGGS

3 tablespoons Red Boat Fish Sauce
¼ pound onion, minced
3 tablespoons Red Boat Palm Sugar
1 tablespoon apple cider vinegar
6 eggs

1. In a small pot, combine the fish sauce, onion, palm sugar, and 2¼ cups cold water.
2. Bring the mixture to a boil, then reduce the heat to low. Simmer for 20 minutes, then remove from the heat. Once cooled, strain and pour the marinade into a quart-size jar.
3. In a medium pot over high heat, bring 2 quarts water and the vinegar to a boil. While the water heats, prepare a bowl of ice water and set aside.
4. Once the water is at a boil, gently add the eggs. Boil the eggs for 7 minutes. Using a slotted spoon, transfer the eggs to the ice bath. Let eggs sit in the iced water for a few minutes, then peel.
5. Add the eggs to the jar of marinade. Make sure they're completely submerged; if necessary, place a small ramekin on top to weigh down the eggs and keep them in the liquid. Place the jar in the fridge. They'll be ready to eat in 4 hours but will taste even better the next day. The eggs can be stored, covered, in the refrigerator for up to 4 days.

CHẢ TRỨNG (EGG MEAT LOAF) TWO WAYS

Both the southern and northern regions of Việt Nam have their own way of making chả trứng and each style has its very ardent fans. The difference between the two lies primarily in how they're cooked: Where northerners pan-fry the mixture, southerners steam it. We're partial to the southern way of making chả trứng, but we wanted to offer both versions for you to try.

CHẢ TRỨNG CHIÊN (FRIED SKILLET EGG MEAT LOAF)

SERVES 4 TO 6

- **1** ounce dried cellophane noodles (see page 22)
- **4** cups hot water, divided
- **½** ounce dried wood ear mushrooms
- **½** pound white or yellow onion, roughly chopped
- **2** tablespoons minced garlic
- **2** tablespoons minced ginger
- **1** pound boneless chicken thighs
- **1** tablespoon Red Boat Fish Sauce
- **2** eggs
- **½** teaspoon ground black pepper
- **3** tablespoons grapeseed, canola, vegetable, or other neutral oil with a high smoke point

FOR SERVING

Steamed rice

Red Boat Scallion Oil (page 285)

All-Purpose Nước Chấm, Điệp Pham's Nước Chấm, or Nước Chấm Gừng (Ginger Dipping Sauce) (pages 275, 277, and 280)

→ *continued*

1. In a small bowl, soak the cellophane noodles in 2 cups of the hot water for 1 to 2 minutes. After 1 minute, the noodles should be soft enough to cut; if not, continue to soak for an additional minute. Drain the softened noodles in a colander and use scissors to cut the noodles into 2-inch strands. Set aside in the colander.
2. In another small bowl, soak the wood ear mushrooms in the remaining 2 cups of hot water for 10 minutes. Drain and rinse the wood ears thoroughly to dislodge any grit, then discard the tough stems. Rough chop the wood ears and set aside in a colander.
3. Combine the onion, garlic, and ginger in a food processor. Add the chopped wood ears and cellophane noodles and process until all the ingredients are finely ground. Remove the mixture and set aside.
4. Chop the chicken thighs into 2-inch pieces, then grind in the food processor. Four pulses should be sufficient to break down the chicken. Add the wood ear–noodle mixture back to the bowl of the food processor, along with the fish sauce. Give the mixture 2 to 3 pulses, just enough to incorporate all the ingredients.
5. Crack the eggs into the processor bowl. Add the pepper and pulse another 2 to 3 times to incorporate the eggs. Remove the mixture and set aside.
6. Heat a 10-inch skillet over medium-high heat. Add the oil, then pour the meat loaf mixture into the hot skillet. The mixture should sizzle when it hits the pan.
7. Use a spatula to flatten out the meat loaf, then lower the flame to medium and cook for 10 minutes to develop the bottom crust.
8. Once the sides of the meat loaf start to brown, give the skillet a firm shake—the meat loaf should loosen from the pan—then slide the meat loaf onto a large plate. Cover the meat loaf with another large plate, facedown, and flip. Remove the top plate and slide the meat loaf, uncooked-side down, back to the skillet. Cook for another 6 minutes on medium heat to develop the crust.
9. Transfer to a large dish and serve with steamed rice, scallion oil, and nước chấm.

You can easily double this recipe and freeze the extra batch for later use. To do so, follow steps 1 through 4, then remove half of the mixture and store in a resealable bag in the freezer for up to 3 months. When you want to make another meat loaf, simply defrost, add the eggs, and proceed with the rest of the recipe. You'll have meat loaf in less than 30 minutes!

→ *continued*

CHẢ TRỨNG HẤP (STEAMED EGG MEAT LOAF)

SERVES 4

1 ounce dried cellophane noodles
2 cups warm water
¼ ounce dried wood ear mushrooms
2 cups hot water
5 scallions, whites and green parts, chopped
1 tablespoon minced garlic
½ pound ground pork
¼ teaspoon ground black pepper
3 teaspoons Red Boat Fish Sauce, divided
½ teaspoon apple cider vinegar
5 eggs, divided
Vegetable or canola oil

FOR SERVING

Steamed rice
Red Boat Scallion Oil (page 285)
All-Purpose Nước Chấm, Điệp Pham's Nước Chấm, or Nước Chấm Gừng (Ginger Dipping Sauce) (pages 275, 277, and 280)

1. In a small bowl, soak the cellophane noodles in the warm water. After 1 minute, the noodles should be soft enough to cut; if not, continue to soak for an additional minute. Drain the softened noodles into a colander and use scissors to cut them into 2-inch strands. Set aside and let drain further.
2. In another small bowl, soak the wood ear mushroom in the hot water for 10 minutes. Drain and rinse the wood ears thoroughly to dislodge any grit. Discard the tough stems, then rough chop the wood ears and set aside in a colander.
3. Place the scallions and garlic in a mini-food processor or the small bowl of your food processor. Add the chopped wood ears and glass noodles and process until all the ingredients are finely ground. Transfer the mixture to a medium mixing bowl.
4. Add the ground pork, pepper, 2½ teaspoons of fish sauce, apple cider vinegar, and 2 eggs to the bowl. Mix to combine the ingredients.
5. Oil an 8-inch cake pan and line the bottom and sides with parchment paper. Pour the pork-and-egg mixture into the pan.
6. Place a steamer rack in a large pot. Fill the pot with 2½ inches of water and bring the water to a hard simmer. Place the cake pan on the steamer rack, cover, and steam for 1 hour.
7. While meat loaf steams, separate the yolks from 2 eggs and place in a bowl. Crack 1 whole egg into the bowl and add the

remaining ½ teaspoon Red Boat Fish Sauce. Whisk to combine.

8. After the meat loaf has steamed for 1 hour, uncover the pot and gently pour in the egg yolk mixture on top of the loaf. Use a spoon to spread the mixture evenly across the top.
9. Return the lid to the pot and steam for another 15 minutes, or until the yolks are set.
10. Remove the meat loaf from the pot and let cool for at least 10 minutes before cutting into wedges. Serve with steamed rice, scallion oil, and nước chấm.

CHAPTER 2

APPETIZERS & SNACKS

CHICKEN WINGS FOR A PARTY

These are the wings you want for a party, marinated in a fish sauce–infused batter, fried to a deeply satisfying crunch. There's enough batter here for about a dozen wings or drumettes, depending on their size, but you can easily double or triple it if you're looking to make a mountain of wings. We serve it here with a buttery dipping sauce, but the wings are also fantastic with nước chấm; try it, for instance, with our All-Purpose Nước Chấm or our Peanut-Coconut Nước Chấm (pages 275 and 281). In either case, once dredged in tapioca starch—which gives the chicken a light and crisp exterior—and fried, they're delicious served piping hot and eaten right away. That said, we've also been known to eat the leftovers straight out of the fridge the next day.

MAKES 10 TO 12 WINGS

WINGS

1 shallot
3 garlic cloves
1 (1-inch) segment ginger
2 tablespoons Red Boat Fish Sauce
1½ tablespoons granulated sugar
1 teaspoon ground black pepper
1½ pounds chicken wings or drumettes, or a combination of both
½ cup tapioca starch
Grapeseed, canola, vegetable, or peanut oil, for frying

BUTTERY DIPPING SAUCE

1 tablespoon butter
½ cup minced white onion
1 tablespoon minced garlic
1 tablespoon granulated sugar
1 teaspoon Red Boat Fish Sauce
1 teaspoon apple cider vinegar

Marinate the wings

1. Use a fine grater to grate the shallot, garlic, and ginger into a small mixing bowl, then transfer to a resealable food storage bag. (You want to grind the three as finely as possible so they won't burn when it's time to fry. If you don't have a Microplane or a grater with fine teeth, you can mash the shallot, garlic, and ginger to a paste in a mortar and pestle instead.)
2. Add the 2 tablespoons fish sauce, sugar, and black pepper to the bag, then add the chicken wings as well. Squeeze out the excess air, then seal the bag. Massage the marinade into the wings and refrigerate for at least 15 minutes, or up to 24 hours.

Make the sauce

3. In a small pot over medium heat, add the butter, onion, and garlic. Sauté the onions and garlic until aromatic.
4. Add 1 cup of water, sugar, 1 teaspoon fish sauce, and vinegar to the pot. Bring the pot to a boil, then lower the heat and simmer for 15 minutes.
5. Strain the sauce and simmer further, until the sauce has thickened slightly and reduced by half. Transfer the sauce to a ramekin.

Fry the wings and serve

6. Place the tapioca starch in a medium mixing bowl. Remove the wings from the marinade and add them to the bowl, tossing to evenly coat them in the starch.
7. Fill a heavy-bottomed pot with 3 inches of oil and place over medium heat. Heat the oil to 350°F on a deep-fry thermometer.
8. Fry the wings in the hot oil, working in batches as necessary to avoid crowding the pot, for 3 minutes. Flip and fry for another 2 to 3 minutes, until golden brown.
9. Transfer wings to a wire rack over a baking sheet to drain. Serve the wings with the buttery dipping sauce.

CHẢ GIÒ TÔM THỊT
(IMPERIAL ROLLS WITH SHRIMP AND PORK)

It's always a good time for an egg roll. Whether it's an informal family weekend get-together or a holiday feast, at least one person comes in with a contribution of egg rolls, complete with plenty of nước chấm and leaves for wrapping. It does take some time to prepare the pork and shrimp filling, to roll the filling in rice paper wrappers, and to fry them all, but it goes by quickly if you have a few hands to help you. This recipe makes more than enough for a large family gathering; even if it's more than you need, make and fry all of them anyway since you've already gone through the trouble of heating up all the oil. Freeze what you don't use for a quick future meal or snack.

MAKES ABOUT 40 EGG ROLLS

FILLING

1 ounce dried wood ear mushrooms

⅓ pound taro root, peeled and roughly chopped

⅓ pound white or yellow onion, roughly chopped

¼ cup grapeseed, canola, vegetable, or other neutral oil, plus additional for frying and sautéing

1 pound ground pork shoulder

1 pound shrimp, peeled, deveined, and coarsely chopped

1¼ cups thinly sliced scallions

1½ tablespoons Red Boat Fish Sauce

½ teaspoon ground white pepper

½ teaspoon ground black pepper

WRAPPING

3 tablespoons granulated sugar

1 packet (6-inch diameter) rice paper wrappers

Grapeseed, canola, vegetable, or peanut oil, for frying

FOR SERVING

1 head lettuce

1 bunch rau răm

1 bunch hot mint

1 bunch cilantro

Perilla leaves

All-Purpose Nước Chấm (page 275)

→ *continued*

Chả Giò Tôm Thịt (Imperial Rolls with Shrimp and Pork) and Taro Shrimp Fritters

Make the filling

1. Soak the wood ear mushrooms in hot water to rehydrate, about 20 minutes. Rinse them well to remove any residual grit. Drain, discard the woody stems, then roughly chop.
2. Grind the mushrooms, taro, and onion in the bowl of a food processor until minced.
3. Heat the oil in a medium skillet over a medium-low flame, then add the minced vegetables. Sauté, stirring constantly, until caramelized, about 15 minutes. Transfer to a large mixing bowl and let cool.
4. Add the remaining filling ingredients and mix to incorporate. Set aside until you're ready to roll.

Make the rolls

5. In a mixing bowl, dissolve the sugar into 2 quarts of hot water.
6. Dip a sheet of rice paper into the hot water, just enough to make it pliable. Shake off the excess water, then place the rice paper on a cutting board. Spread 1½ tablespoons of the filling across the bottom center of the rice paper. Fold in the left and right sides so that they almost meet in the middle and nearly cover all the filling. Starting at the bottom, roll up the rice paper. The egg roll should resemble a small cigar.
7. Set the roll, seam-side down, on a large plate or baking sheet, and repeat with the remainder of the filling.

Fry and serve the rolls

8. Fill a cast-iron skillet or heavy-bottomed pan with at least 4 inches of oil. Heat the oil to 325°F on a deep-fry thermometer.
9. Working in batches, carefully place a few egg rolls in the oil, being sure not to crowd the skillet. The high moisture content of the uncooked rolls will cause the oil to sputter and bubble. Turn the rolls frequently in the oil so they fry evenly on all sides. Fry for 5 minutes, then use tongs to gently pry apart any rolls that are stuck together.
10. When the many bubbles around the rolls subside to just a few, that's an indication that the filling is cooked through. To test if the shells are properly crisped, use tongs to squeeze the rolls. If the rolls yield to the pressure, continue frying until the chả giò shell is hard and crisp, then remove them from the oil and let drain on a wire rack set inside a baking sheet. Fry the remaining rolls.
11. To serve, place the egg rolls on a large platter and set on the table with the herbs and nước chấm.

To freeze any leftover rolls, arrange them in a single layer on a wire rack set on top of a baking sheet. Place the entire baking sheet in the freezer to chill for an hour. When the rolls are frozen, transfer them to a freezer bag. The egg rolls will keep in the freezer for up to a year. To reheat, preheat the oven to 350°F. Place the frozen rolls on a wire rack on top of a baking sheet and bake for 20 to 30 minutes, until the rolls are hot and crisp.

TARO SHRIMP FRITTERS

These fritters, aromatic with garlic and turmeric, are a riff on the classic Hà Nội street snack called bánh tôm, in which shrimp or prawns are nestled in a basket of sweet potato, then fried. We swap out the sweet potato for taro here for a slightly different flavor; the taro is also lower in moisture than sweet potato, so the fritters stay crisp longer. You can use any size shrimp, though larger shrimp will be easier to slice and offer a more dramatic presentation than smaller shrimp. While these fritters do indeed make great snacks, you can also turn them into a family-style meal by serving them with a platter of lettuce, herbs, and rice paper wrappers. In either case, you will definitely want to dip these in plenty of nước chấm. If you don't already have a jar in the fridge, you can easily make the nước chấm in the time it takes for the oil to reach the proper frying temperature.

MAKES AT LEAST 12 FRITTERS

FOR THE FRITTERS

1 teaspoon baking soda
1½ tablespoons kosher salt
½ pound peeled and deveined shrimp
½ pound taro, shredded
⅓ cup tapioca starch
1 tablespoon minced garlic
1½ teaspoons Red Boat Fish Sauce
1 teaspoon granulated sugar
1 teaspoon minced Thai chile, seeds and ribs removed if desired
½ teaspoon ground turmeric

Canola, peanut, rice bran, or grapeseed oil, for frying

→ *continued*

FOR SERVING

AS HORS D'OEUVRES

½ cup All-Purpose Nước Chấm (page 275) or Nước Chấm Me (Tamarind Dipping Sauce) (page 282)

AS A FAMILY-STYLE ENTREE

Lettuce
1 bunch cilantro
1 bunch Thai basil
1 bunch mint
Perilla leaves
Rice paper wrappers
½ cup All-Purpose Nước Chấm (page 275) or Nước Chấm Me (Tamarind Dipping Sauce) (page 282)

Make the fritters

1. In a medium mixing bowl, dissolve the baking soda and salt in 2 cups water. Add the shrimp and let them sit in the brine in the refrigerator for 15 to 30 minutes.
2. Combine the taro, tapioca starch, garlic, fish sauce, sugar, chile, turmeric, and ¼ cup water in a bowl. Mix the ingredients to create a thin batter, then set aside.
3. Drain the shrimp, then dry between paper towels. Set aside six of the plumpest shrimp and mince the remaining ones. Combine the minced shrimp with the batter. Stir to coat all the ingredients, then place the bowl in the refrigerator until you're ready to fry.
4. Halve the six reserved shrimp lengthwise. Put in the refrigerator, covered, until ready to fry.

Fry the fritters

5. If not serving right away, preheat the oven to 150°F.
6. Fill a deep, heavy-bottomed skillet or pot with 2 inches of oil. (Choose a skillet or pot that is at least 4 inches high, so that there is at least 2 inches of clearance from the top of the oil and the lip of the pan.)
7. Heat the oil to 325°F on a deep-fry thermometer. When it reaches temperature, pour ¼ cup of the fritter batter into a wide, shallow metal ladle. Press a halved shrimp onto the top of the fritter. Gently slip the fritter into the oil. Fry on each side for 1 to 2 minutes, until golden and crisp. While frying, keep an eye on the temperature of the oil: It shouldn't go above 325°F, nor drop below 300°F. Fry the fritters in batches to help stabilize the oil's temperature, about three fritters at a time, and wait for the oil to return to 325°F between each batch.
8. Once the fritters are golden, remove them from the oil and let drain on a wire rack set over a baking sheet. If not serving immediately, place the rack in a warm oven to keep the fritters hot and crisp. Serve with nước chấm and, if serving family style, lettuce, herbs, and rice paper wrappers.

PHÚ QUỐC SARDINE SALAD

This dish is a take on cá trích, a specialty of Phú Quốc that is popular throughout the island. The star is the humble sardine. After a light pickle in lime juice and a toss with freshly shredded coconut, peanuts, and herbs, the fish is rolled in rice paper and served with a sweet coconut nước chấm. We've especially enjoyed this salad at a few beachside restaurants, and we've found noshing on these summer rolls with our feet in the sand and a bucket of ice cold beer within arm's reach as the sun sets is one of the most relaxing, satisfying ways to spend an evening in Phú Quốc. Because it requires no cooking at all, it's also perfect to throw together when the weather is too hot to fire up the stove or oven. With so few components, the quality of the ingredients will make all the difference, so source the freshest coconut and sardines you can find. If you can't find suitable sardines, yellowtail is an excellent substitution.

SERVES 4 TO 6

FISH

½ pound sardine or yellowtail fillets, sliced ¼ inch thick
1 cup lime juice
¼ pound red onion, thinly sliced
⅓ cup grated fresh coconut flesh (from a mature coconut; see sidebar, page 59)
⅓ cup unsalted roasted peanuts, ground
½ cup rau răm leaves, minced

DRESSING

1 tablespoon minced garlic
1 to **2** Thai chiles, seeds and ribs removed if desired, minced
¼ teaspoon granulated sugar
2 tablespoons lime juice
1 teaspoon Red Boat Fish Sauce

FOR SERVING

Peanut-Coconut Nước Chấm (page 281)
Rice paper wrappers
1 head butter lettuce
1 bunch rau răm
1 bunch cilantro
1 stack perilla leaves

→ *continued*

1. In a mixing bowl, gently mix together the fish fillets with the 1 cup lime juice. Place the bowl in the refrigerator and marinate for 30 minutes to 1 hour.
2. Meanwhile, make the dressing: Combine the garlic, 1 chile, sugar, 2 tablespoons lime juice, and fish sauce in a small bowl or jar. Stir to dissolve the sugar. Taste and see if you like the level of heat; if you'd like it spicier, add some or all of the second chile.
3. Remove the sardines from the refrigerator. Drain and discard the lime juice, then transfer the sardines to a clean mixing bowl.
4. Add the red onion, grated coconut, peanuts, and rau răm to the sardines, then pour the dressing over all and gently toss to coat. Transfer the sardine salad to a platter.
5. To serve, start by giving each guest their own small dipping bowl of peanut-coconut nước chấm. Place the salad on the table along with a plate of rice paper wrappers and herbs, and encourage everyone to assemble their own summer rolls.

HOW TO CRACK A FRESH MATURE COCONUT AND EXTRACT COCONUT WATER

When shopping, you'll likely to run across mature and young coconuts. They're easy to tell apart: Young coconuts have a spongy, soft white exterior while mature coconuts have a brown, dry husk. For this recipe, a fresh, mature coconut is key, as its firm flesh stands up well to the salad dressing.

One coconut will yield more flesh and water than you'll need for this recipe, but both freeze well.

To crack open a coconut, soak it first in cold water for 30 minutes. Then, while holding the coconut over an empty bowl, use a hammer and tap along the equator of the coconut until it cracks. The bowl will catch the coconut water that is released.

To extract the juicy flesh of the coconut and collect all its water, use the hammer to continue cracking along the middle until it cracks in half. Run a butter knife between the flesh of the coconut and the shell and pull the flesh away from the shell. (Older coconuts may take a little extra elbow grease to pry the meat away.) Use a grater to grate the coconut flesh or finely mince it with a knife.

BLISTERED SUMMER VEGETABLES WITH SCALLION OIL

Corn is at its sweetest between June and late September, right around the same time okra and zucchini and other summer squash also are at the height of their flavors. To celebrate these summer vegetables, we blister them in hot oil so their natural sugars caramelize, then douse them in our fish sauce–infused scallion oil to make an appetizer that is crunchy, sweet, and salty all at the same time. To really make the most of this recipe, choose squash that is firm and dense—the less water content, the better they'll blister. You can use these techniques to blister pretty much any vegetable in your summer garden, from tomatoes to eggplant. And if you already have the grill going, you can blister the vegetables there rather than frying them.

SERVES 6 TO 8

Canola, vegetable, peanut, or grapeseed oil, for frying
4 ears corn, shucked and cut into 3-inch segments if desired
½ pound okra
½ pound summer squash
Red Boat Scallion Oil (page 285)

1. Fill a large Dutch oven with 3 inches of oil. Bring the oil to 380°F on a deep-fry thermometer.
2. Line a baking sheet with a wire rack. Add the corn cobs to the oil, working in batches if necessary to avoid overcrowding. Cover the pot with a splatter screen. Fry for 2 to 3 minutes, just until the kernels start to blister and caramelize, then carefully transfer them to the prepared baking sheet to drain. Repeat with the remaining corn, okra, and squash.
3. Transfer all the blistered vegetables to a platter and top with plenty of scallion oil. Serve.

THE RED BOAT CHEF COMMUNITY

Soon after I launched Red Boat, I got a call from Le Bernardin in New York, asking me how they could source Red Boat for the restaurant. That was a complete surprise. When I launched Red Boat, I was so focused on getting it right for my mom, and home cooks like my mom, that it didn't occur to me that chefs might be interested in what I was doing. I shipped Le Bernardin a few bottles of Red Boat and, as far as I know, Le Bernardin was the first restaurant to use our fish sauce.

That shipment marked the beginning of Red Boat's relationship with chefs across the country. Indeed, Diep Tran also looked us up soon after she opened her restaurant, Good Girl Dinette. (She closed her restaurant in 2018 and has since joined us as our R&D chef!) Bryant Ng at Cassia in Santa Monica, and Stuart Brioza and Nicole Krasinski, the chefs and owners of State Bird Provisions and The Progress in San Francisco, also were among the earliest supporters of my vision for Red Boat.

Over the years, we have been fortunate to meet so many other chefs who are enthusiastic about the flavor of our fish sauce and have chosen to use it in their restaurant kitchens. And because we catch, salt, ferment, and bottle our fish sauce, we are constantly connecting with chefs who are interested in traceability. A few chefs have dropped by our barrel house while traveling through Việt Nam, and I've loved the opportunity to host and to show how we make our fish sauce.

A few of our chef friends have been kind enough to share recipes with us to include in this book. The following recipe, from Justin Chao at Le Bon Garçon, is the first. In later pages, you'll find recipes from Bryant, Stuart, and Nicole, as well as Christine Hà, *MasterChef* winner and executive chef at The Blind Goat in Houston; Braden and Yasmin Wages, the proprietors of three locations of Malai Kitchen in and around Dallas; and Khánh Ngô, a private chef in Orange County. We hope you enjoy these recipes as much as we do.

LE BON GARÇON'S
RED BOAT BRIC-A-BRAC

This sweet and salty party snack is the brainchild of Justin Chao. Justin is the founder of Le Bon Garçon in Los Angeles, a confectionary that produces a creative variety of ever-changing caramels, including the classic French-style salted caramel. We first approached Justin to develop a caramel using Red Boat Salt and Red Boat Palm Sugar. This process involved Justin shipping several different versions of his experimental caramels to us to taste. In one shipment he included a tiny bag of a treat he made on a whim: rice squares coated in melted Red Boat Salted Caramel. Once we tried it, our entire team couldn't get enough. We ended up working with him on not just the Red Boat Salted Caramels, but also on this snack, which we call Bric-a-Brac. He was kind enough to adapt his recipe for the home kitchen.

MAKES ABOUT 4 CUPS

1 (17-ounce) box rice squares cereal
¼ cup whole milk
1¾ cups (14 ounces) Red Boat Palm Sugar, divided
½ cup corn syrup
½ pound butter, cut into 2-inch cubes
Cayenne pepper (optional)
1 tablespoon Red Boat Salt

1. Preheat oven to 250°F. Line two baking sheets with parchment paper or Silpat baking mats.
2. Pour half of the cereal onto one baking sheet, being sure to spread it out in a single layer. Repeat with the other half of the cereal on the second baking sheet.
3. Combine the milk and ¼ cup (2 ounces) of the palm sugar in a microwavable bowl, then microwave for 30 seconds. Remove the bowl and whisk until the palm sugar dissolves. Set aside.
4. Add the corn syrup to the milk mixture and stir until the corn syrup dissolves.
5. Pour 1½ cups of water into a 3½-quart saucepan. Add the remaining 1½ cups palm sugar and bring to a boil.
6. When the sugar begins to brown, after about 20 minutes, turn off the heat and let the caramel darken. When the caramel becomes a mahogany red, add the milk mixture. The addition of the milk will harden the caramel.
7. Turn the heat to medium and whisk the mixture until the caramelized sugar dissolves. Slowly add the cubes of butter, whisking constantly to blend the butter into the caramel.
8. Keep the saucepan at a simmer over medium heat until it has thickened slightly, about 90 seconds, then whisk in a pinch of cayenne pepper (if using) and the salt.
9. Remove the caramel from the heat and pour half of the sauce onto the cereal on one baking sheet. Stir everything with a silicone spatula until the cereal is coated. Spread the cereal into thin layer. Repeat with the other half of the caramel sauce and the cereal on the second baking sheet.
10. Bake the cereal in the oven for 1 hour and 45 minutes. Stir the mix every 30 minutes with a silicone spatula, making sure to scrape up and mix back in any caramel that has pooled at the bottom of the pan.
11. When the caramel has darkened and thickened, take one baking sheet out of oven and stir the mixture again to separate the individual pieces of cereal. Carefully spoon the hot cereal mix into a bowl. Repeat with the second baking sheet.
12. Set aside the bowls and let the mix cool, giving each bowl a good stir occasionally to help it cool down. When the mix has cooled and become crunchy, it's ready to eat.

CHAPTER 3

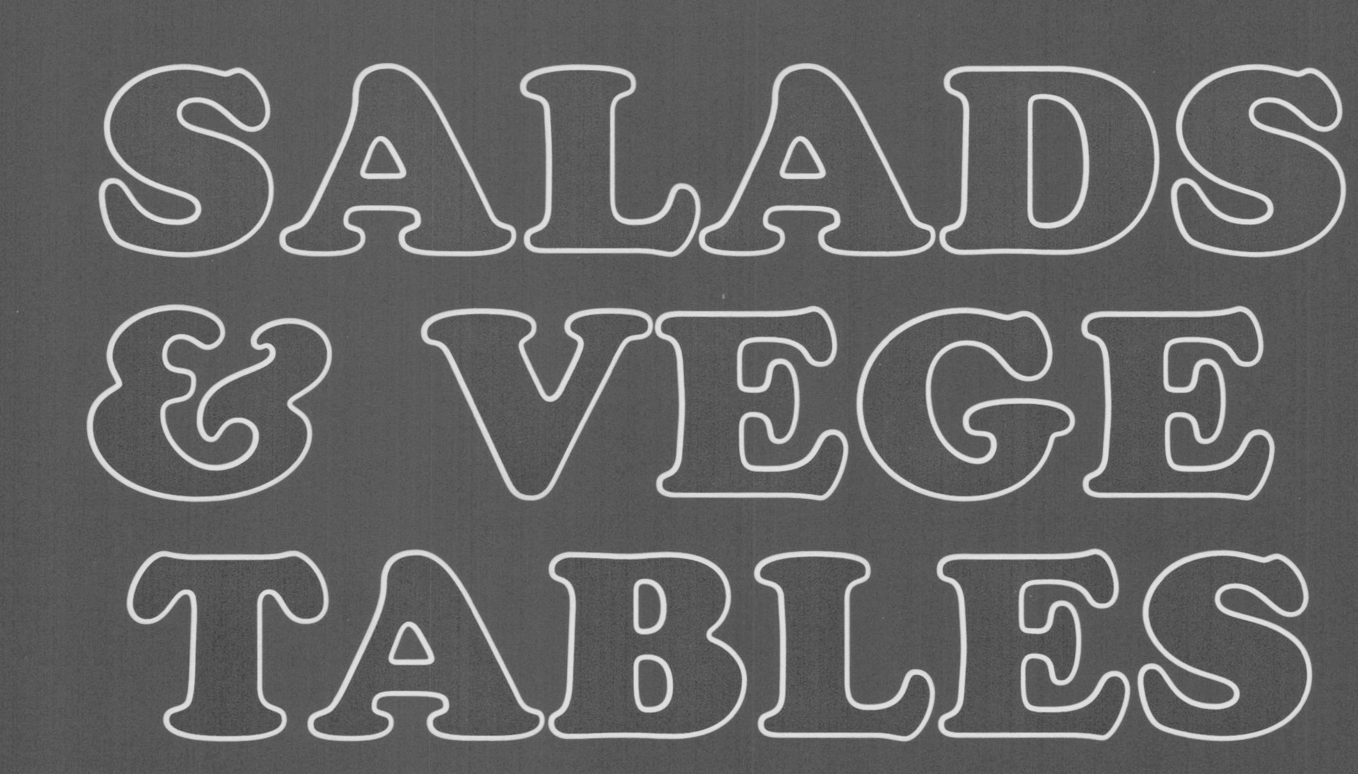

CAESAR SALAD WITH HERBED BREAD CRUMBS

Caesar salad dressings often incorporate a few powerhouse umami ingredients like Parmesan cheese, anchovy fillets, and Worcestershire sauce. For our version of this classic, we've opted to swap out the anchovies and the Worcestershire in favor of a few solid glugs of our fish sauce. The substitution works in large part because our fish sauce is made with wild-caught black anchovies, and those anchovies are not only deeply flavorful, they also pack quite a bit of umami. (Using the fish sauce here is especially convenient if you don't always have anchovies on hand.) Combined with the natural umami in the Parmesan and eggs, the dressing just pops. Right before serving, we shower the salad with our Herbed Bread Crumbs (page 86), which are also flavored with a bit of fish sauce. If you have yet to regularly reach for the fish sauce in your cooking, this recipe is a great way to introduce you to the myriad ways it can be used in your kitchen.

SERVES 4 TO 6

DRESSING

1 small garlic clove, smashed
1 tablespoon Dijon mustard
2 tablespoons grated Parmigiano-Reggiano
2 tablespoons Red Boat Fish Sauce, plus up to 2 teaspoons to taste
¼ cup champagne vinegar
¼ teaspoon ground black pepper
1 whole egg plus 1 egg yolk
1 cup grapeseed oil

SALAD

3 romaine hearts, washed and dried
½ cup toasted and chopped cashews
Herbed Bread Crumbs (page 86) or croutons

Make the dressing

1. In a mason jar, add the garlic, mustard, cheese, 2 tablespoons fish sauce, champagne vinegar, and black pepper. Use an immersion blender to puree the mixture into a smooth paste, about 1 minute.
2. Once the paste is smooth, add the whole egg and egg yolk. Blend for 30 to 60 seconds, until the egg is emulsified into the paste.
3. With the blender still running, slowly add the oil. Blend until all the oil is incorporated. Taste and add up to 2 more teaspoons of the fish sauce if you'd like.
4. Store the dressing in the refrigerator until ready to use. The dressing will thicken as it sits in the refrigerator.

Assemble the salad

5. Separate the romaine leaves and place them in a large mixing bowl. Add ½ to ¾ cup of the dressing. Toss to coat the leaves, and add more dressing if necessary.
6. Divide the greens among serving bowls or plates. Sprinkle some cashews and bread crumbs on each salad. Serve.

SHRIMP AND GREEN BEANS

Shrimp and green beans is one of Ann's dinner staples. It's a dish that comes together incredibly quickly: The shrimp is marinated in a combination of fish sauce and oyster sauce, but just briefly. Meanwhile, the beans are blanched, and finally the shrimp and the beans are sautéed together, but just for all of 5 minutes. This makes it perfect for any night of the week, but especially a busy weeknight when you need to get something tasty and healthy on the table fast. If you anticipate a very busy week and find yourself with more green beans and shrimp than you need for this recipe, you can blanch all the beans at once and they will keep fresh, in the fridge, for up to four days. When you're ready, all you have to do is marinate the shrimp and rewarm the beans, and you'll have a very easy meal ready in no time at all.

SERVES 4

½ pound large fresh shrimp, peeled and deveined
1 teaspoon oyster sauce
2 teaspoons Red Boat Fish Sauce, plus additional to taste
1 tablespoon kosher salt
1 pound green beans
4 teaspoons vegetable oil
½ pound yellow onion, sliced into thin wedges
1 garlic clove, minced

GARNISH

1 small bunch cilantro, chopped
Ground black pepper

1. In a medium bowl, toss the shrimp with the oyster sauce and fish sauce. Mix to combine and set aside to marinate.
2. Fill a large pot with 2 quarts of water, add the salt, and set over high heat. While you wait for the water to come to a boil, prepare an ice bath by filling a large bowl with ice and water.
3. When the water in the pot reaches a boil, drop in the green beans. Cook for 30 seconds, then use a wire strainer or tongs to transfer the beans to the ice bath. Let the beans sit in the ice bath for 5 minutes to stop the cooking process and preserve their bright color, then drain in a colander. Trim the stem ends and return to the colander to continue to drain.
4. In a large pan over high heat, heat the oil. When the oil shimmers, it's time to sauté: Working quickly, toss in the sliced onion and sauté for 1 minute, shaking and stirring the pan constantly throughout. Add the minced garlic and sauté just until the garlic becomes aromatic, 20 to 30 seconds. Add the marinated shrimp and sauté until they start to curl slightly, about 2 minutes. Add the green beans to the pan and sauté for another 3 minutes, or until the beans have warmed and the shrimp is opaque and cooked through. Taste, and add an additional drizzle of fish sauce if needed. Transfer to a serving plate and garnish with cilantro and ground black pepper.

STUFFED BITTER MELON SOUP

This is one of our favorite soups to make at home, although the kids didn't acquire the taste for it until they were a bit older. If you're not familiar with bitter melon, you'll find the long, knobby-skinned fruit at Asian markets and, depending on where you live, you may be able to source it at your local farmers market, too. They may be white or green in color, with the green bitter melon turning a sunset orange as it matures. Bitter melon is indeed bitter—but not significantly more so than, say, the bitterness in coffee. (I actually prefer the most bitter of bitter melons!) Here, the bitterness of the vegetable is tempered by the rich pork filling and the sweetness of the coconut soda. The filling calls for fish paste, which you can find in the frozen aisle of most Asian supermarkets.

SERVES 4 TO 6

MEAT FILLING

¾ ounce cellophane noodles

½ ounce dried wood ear mushrooms

2 tablespoons minced shallots

⅓ cup thinly sliced scallions, white root end only

½ teaspoon granulated sugar

2 teaspoons ground black pepper

½ teaspoon oyster sauce

1 teaspoon sesame oil

1 pound ground pork

½ cup fish paste

2 tablespoons Red Boat Fish Sauce

BITTER MELON

2 pounds bitter melon

2 (12-ounce) cans coconut soda

1 bunch cilantro, stems and leaves separated

3 Thai chiles (optional)

3 to **4** tablespoons Red Boat Fish Sauce, divided

⅓ cup thinly sliced scallions, green tops only

FOR SERVING

Steamed rice

Red Boat Fish Sauce

→ *continued*

Start the filling

1. In a small bowl, soak the cellophane noodles in 2 cups of hot water for 1 to 2 minutes. Drain in a colander and use scissors to cut the noodles into 1-inch strands. Set aside and let the noodles drain further in the colander.
2. In another small bowl, soak the wood ear mushrooms in 2 cups of hot water for 10 minutes. Drain and rinse thoroughly to dislodge any grit and discard the tough stems. Mince and set aside in a colander to continue draining.

Prepare the melon

3. Cut and discard the ends of the bitter melons, then slice each into 1-inch segments. Use a butter knife to cut out the core of each segment, then run the knife along the inner walls to scrape away as much of the bitter white pith as possible.
4. Bring 2 quarts water to a boil in large pot, then add the melon segments. Boil for 2 minutes, then drain in colander.
5. In a mixing bowl, combine the cellophane noodles, wood ear, and the rest of the meat filling ingredients. Work and knead the meat mixture until all the ingredients are evenly incorporated, 2 to 4 minutes.
6. Stuff the cavity of each melon segment with the filling. Compress the filling between the palms of your hands, flattening it so it completely fills the cavity and is flush with each side of the segment (this will prevent the filling from falling out when they cook).
7. Place the stuffed bitter melon on a baking sheet. Form any remaining meat filling into mini-meatballs and add them to the baking sheet. Cover the sheet with plastic wrap and put in the refrigerator for 10 minutes.
8. While the meat rests in the refrigerator, combine the coconut soda, 1½ quarts water, cilantro stems, and chiles (if using) in a large stockpot. Bring to a simmer over medium heat and simmer for 10 minutes.
9. Add the stuffed bitter melon and meatballs to the pot. Increase the heat and bring the pot to a boil, then reduce the heat and simmer for 30 minutes, skimming off any impurities that rise to the surface. Remove the cilantro stems after 15 minutes of simmering.
10. After 30 minutes of simmering, poke a chopstick through a bitter melon segment. If the chopstick easily pierces the bitter melon, it is done. If not, continue simmering for another 5 to 10 minutes.
11. Turn off the heat. Add 3 tablespoons of fish sauce to the pot. Taste and add up to 1 more tablespoon if you feel the broth isn't salty enough.
12. Garnish the soup with scallion tops and cilantro leaves. Serve with rice and fish sauce for dipping.

BROCCOLINI WITH VERY DELICIOUS GARLIC SAUCE

If you ever need help eating your greens, try tossing them in this delicious combination of fish sauce and garlic. You'll make more sauce than you'll need for this recipe, but it's so delicious that we're sure you'll find other ways to use it. We use broccolini here, but it also goes very well with spinach, collards, cabbage, or bok choy. Store the extra sauce in an airtight container in the refrigerator for up to 10 days. It's ready to use, right out of the fridge or re-warmed, on your next plate of leafy greens.

SERVES 4

¼ cup (about 6 cloves) minced garlic

¼ cup grapeseed, canola, vegetable, or other neutral oil

1½ tablespoons Red Boat Fish Sauce

2 teaspoons sesame oil

1 tablespoon kosher salt

1 pound broccolini, cut into 2-inch pieces

Make the garlic sauce

1. In a small saucepan over medium-low heat, combine the garlic and oil. Cook until the garlic starts to turn a pale golden color, stirring frequently to ensure the garlic toasts evenly, 7 to 10 minutes.
2. Transfer the garlic and its oil to a jar or bowl. Stir in the fish sauce and sesame oil, then set aside while you blanch the broccolini.

Blanch the broccolini

3. In a large pot over high heat, bring 4 quarts of water and the salt to a boil. While the water heats, fill a bowl with ice water and place next to your stove.
4. Working in batches, add a third of the broccolini to the boiling water. Blanch until cooked through, about 60 seconds. To see if it's cooked enough, carefully bite into a stem. If the center of the stem is still raw, cook for another 30 to 60 seconds. Drain the broccolini and immediately place in the bowl of ice water to arrest the cooking.
5. Let the water come to a boil again before repeating with the remaining broccolini.
6. Once all the broccolini is blanched, set aside in a coriander to drain for 10 to 15 minutes, then dry with paper towels, if necessary. You want the broccolini to be as dry as possible so the dressing will adhere.

Dress and serve the broccolini

7. When you're ready to serve, stir the dressing well to evenly redistribute the ingredients. Drizzle 1 to 2 teaspoons of the garlic sauce over the broccolini. Toss to coat, then taste and add more sauce to your liking. Serve.

If you use a more delicate green like bok choy or cabbage, blanch it for 30 to 60 seconds, or just until tender.

RAU MUỐNG XÀO (MORNING GLORY WITH GARLIC)

When you need a side of vegetables in no time at all, this classic is the perfect dish. If you're not familiar, rau muống is a bright leafy green that's sometimes labeled as morning glory or Vietnamese water spinach at the market. More and more small-scale producers are growing it, too, so look for it the next time you're shopping at your local farmers market. The dish is seasoned with fish sauce and stir-fried with garlic just long enough to cook the greens, and no longer, as overcooking will cause the hollow stems to collapse and lose their crunch. We make rau muống xào often, as it goes with almost everything. Try it alongside any kho (page 90), or pair it with a platter of crispy pork belly (page 87).

SERVES 3 TO 4

10 ounces morning glory
1 teaspoon kosher salt
2 tablespoons vegetable oil
4 garlic cloves, minced
2 teaspoons Red Boat Fish Sauce
1 Thai chile, seeds and ribs removed if desired, minced

Prepare the morning glory

1. Separate the tender morning glory leaves and stems from the hollow main stems. Set aside.
2. Use a paring knife to split the hollow stems into thin strips. Alternatively, cut the hollow stems into 2-inch segments.
3. Pour 4 quarts of water into a large pot, add the salt, and bring to a boil.
4. While the water boils, prepare a bowl of ice water and place it next to the stove.
5. When the water begins to boil, add the hollow stems to the pot and blanch for 20 seconds. Remove them and plunge directly into the ice water to arrest the cooking.
6. Add the tender leaves and stems to the pot of water. Blanch for 10 seconds, then remove and plunge into ice water as well.
7. Keep the morning glory in the iced water for 10 minutes, then drain in a colander for another 10 minutes, shaking the colander often to speed up the drying process.

Sauté the morning glory

8. In a medium sauté pan, add the oil and minced garlic. Over a low flame, slowly heat the oil until the garlic becomes aromatic and begins to caramelize, about 5 minutes.
9. When the garlic starts to caramelize, turn the heat to high and add the morning glory, fish sauce, and minced chile. Sauté for another 5 minutes.
10. Transfer the morning glory to a large serving plate, pouring the pan sauce over the greens.

NOT-SO-VEGETARIAN ĐỒ CHAY

(TOFU AND VEGETABLE BRAISE)

Ann's mother was a lifelong vegetarian, and one of the dishes that she passed down to Ann was đồ chay, a vegetarian braise of tofu and a colorful medley of vegetables. Ann continues to make đồ chay at least once a month, much to Tracy and Tiffany's delight. We've modified the recipe to include fish sauce, which lends the braise a bit of extra savoriness. For the vegetables, Ann uses bitter melon, chayote, carrots, and mushrooms; each has their own cooking time, so she cooks them separately first before tossing everything together. If you don't happen to have all of the above on hand, don't let that stop you: Once you master the basics of making the braise, you can easily adapt it to what you have in your fridge and the personal preferences of your family or guests. Both Tracy and Tiffany have a habit of hoarding all the mushrooms, for instance, so you'll want to add extra if you also have mushroom lovers in your family! We also like to include chả lụa chay, or the vegetarian version of chả lụa, the Vietnamese ham that you often see stuffed in bánh mì; you can find it in the refrigerated section at many Asian markets. Instead of chả lụa chay, you can add additional tofu or vegetables instead. Serve this family style, with a spread of other dishes, and plenty of steamed rice for the table.

→ *continued*

SERVES 6 TO 8

½ pound firm tofu
1 pound bitter melon
1 tablespoon kosher salt
¼ pound chả lụa chay (vegetarian ham)
1 pound chayote, peeled
1 medium carrot, peeled
1½ pounds king oyster mushrooms
¼ cup plus 2 tablespoons vegetable oil, divided
½ cup minced leek, white and light green parts only
2 tablespoons oyster sauce
1 teaspoon soy sauce
1 teaspoon Red Boat Fish Sauce
Ground black pepper
¼ teaspoon granulated sugar

1. Drain the tofu for 1 to 2 hours, then pat dry with a paper towel. Slice the tofu into ½-inch slices.

Be sure the tofu is as dry as possible. This extra step will minimize the splattering when the tofu is fried.

2. Halve the bitter melon lengthwise, then use a spoon to scrape away the white membrane and seeds. Cut the bitter melon into 1-inch pieces and place the pieces in a resealable bag with the kosher salt. Shake to coat the pieces with the salt, then let the bitter melon sit in the salt. After 20 minutes, drain and rinse the pieces. Squeeze the bitter melon pieces to remove as much water as possible, then set aside in a colander to further drain.

3. While the bitter melon drains, prepare the vegetarian ham and vegetables: Cube the vegetarian ham, chayote, and carrot into 1-inch pieces. Brush the mushrooms to remove any grit, then cut the mushrooms into 1-inch pieces, separating the stems from the caps.
4. In a large dry skillet, sauté the bitter melon for 5 minutes, stirring constantly. Remove the bitter melon and set aside.
5. Set the same pan over medium heat and add 2 tablespoons of vegetable oil. When a drop of water sizzles in the pan, the oil is hot enough to add the tofu. Reduce the heat to medium-low and fry for 1½ minutes, until a golden skin forms. Flip the tofu and repeat on the other side. Remove to a plate and remove the pan from the heat. When the tofu slices have cooled enough to handle, slice them into thirds. Set aside.
6. Add 2 tablespoons of vegetable oil to the pan and set over medium heat. When the oil is hot, add the vegetarian ham. Stir-fry the ham until it's slightly caramelized. Set aside.
7. Return the pan over medium heat and add the remaining 2 tablespoons of vegetable oil. When the oil is hot, add the leek and stir-fry until slightly caramelized, golden, and fragrant, about 2 minutes.
8. Add the oyster sauce, soy sauce, fish sauce, a generous pinch of black pepper, and sugar. Stir to combine, then return the tofu and vegetarian ham to the pan. Mix to evenly coat the tofu in the sauce, then remove the tofu and set aside.
9. Add the mushroom stems, chayote, and carrots to the pan along with ½ cup of water. Cover and let the vegetables steam for 8 minutes, then uncover and add the bitter melon and mushroom caps. Cook uncovered until the carrots are cooked but still crisp, about 8 minutes.
10. Return the tofu to the pan and cook just enough to warm the tofu, about 5 minutes. Transfer everything to a serving platter and serve.

PASTA MARINARA

The secret to this pasta marinara is quite literally in the sauce. A few dashes of fish sauce added to pasta sauce has long been the secret ingredient for many a Vietnamese cook, including my mom. The fish sauce gives it that extra *oomph* of flavor that someone who isn't wise to the secret can taste but can't quite place. That it works so well isn't too surprising: There is, after all, a long tradition of cooks stirring slivers of anchovies into their simmering tomato sauces for that very same effect. And, in case anyone asks, the secret to the herbed bread crumbs? Also fish sauce.

SERVES 4 TO 6

MARINARA

2 tablespoons butter
1 tablespoon extra-virgin olive oil
2 cups minced white or yellow onions
2 tablespoons sliced garlic
1 tablespoon Red Boat Fish Sauce
½ teaspoon ground black pepper
1 (28-ounce) can crushed tomatoes
1½ pounds cooked pasta, preferably a strand variety like spaghetti, linguine, or fettuccini

FOR SERVING

Parmigiano-Reggiano
Ground black pepper
Herbed Bread Crumbs (recipe follows)

→ *continued*

1. In a medium saucepot over medium heat, heat the butter and olive oil.
2. When the butter starts to sizzle, add the onions and sauté until they're aromatic, 3 to 5 minutes.
3. Add the garlic and cook until aromatic, 3 to 5 minutes.
4. Lower the heat to low and braise the onions and garlic for 15 minutes, stirring often to prevent the bottom from scorching.
5. Add the fish sauce, black pepper, and crushed tomatoes. Bring to a boil, then reduce the heat to low and simmer for 20 minutes. The total cooking time for the sauce will be 40 to 45 minutes.
6. Over high heat, bring the tomato sauce back to a boil. Add the pasta and cook until it's warmed through, 3 to 5 minutes.
7. Transfer the pasta to bowls and top each bowl with grated Parmesan, black pepper, and bread crumbs.

HERBED BREAD CRUMBS

MAKES 1½ CUPS

2 tablespoons extra-virgin olive oil
1 tablespoon butter
1 teaspoon Red Boat Fish Sauce
1½ cups bread crumbs
1 tablespoon minced garlic
3 tablespoons lemon zest
½ cup minced parsley

1. In a small pan over medium heat, heat the oil, butter, and fish sauce. Once the butter begins to sizzle, add the bread crumbs. Stir to coat evenly in the butter and oil.
2. Take the pan off the heat and mix in the garlic. Transfer the bread crumbs to a mixing bowl to cool.
3. Once the bread crumbs are cool, stir in the lemon zest and parsley. The bread crumbs are ready to use. Any leftovers can be stored in a tightly covered jar for up to 3 days.

STUART BRIOZA'S

FRIED PORK BELLY WITH CITRUS AND HERBS

State Bird Provisions in San Francisco is one of our family's favorite restaurants, and I am so happy to know the restaurant's chefs and owners, Stuart Brioza and Nicole Krasinski. Our friendship began in 2013, when Stuart visited us at the barrel house, and his support for Red Boat helped give me confidence that I was on the right path early on, when sales were slow. Since then, we've worked together on a few fun projects, including a Spiced Garum Salt blend.

This recipe for a vibrant, refreshing citrus salad with braised and fried pork belly was inspired by his trip to Phú Quốc all those years ago. It will require a bit of planning, as Stuart brines the pork for three days before braising it. You can, however, braise the belly up to 3 months in advance and store it in your freezer until needed; the dressing, too, can be made a few days ahead. After you've made the salad, all that's left to do is to fry the belly so it yields the most satisfying crunch.

SERVES 6 TO 8

Rice bran, vegetable, or canola oil, for deep-frying
2 pounds Braised Pork Belly (recipe follows), cut into approximately 1½-inch cubes, chilled
2 cups cornstarch
Kosher salt
2 pounds various citrus, peeled, cut into suprêmes and then into bite-size pieces
1 medium jalapeño chile, seeds included, very thinly sliced
1½ cups loosely packed mixed fresh herbs (such as mint, cilantro, Thai basil, and bronze fennel fronds)
1 cup Fish Sauce Vinaigrette (recipe follows)
2 Indonesian long peppercorns

→ *continued*

1. Line a baking sheet with several layers of paper towels. Pour 3 inches of oil into a large heavy pot and bring to 335°F on a deep-fry thermometer over high heat.
2. Combine the pork belly and cornstarch in a large mixing bowl and toss to coat the cubes well.
3. Fry the pork in several batches, until the belly is brown and crispy, about 5 to 8 minutes per batch. Avoid crowding the pot. As it's fried, transfer the pork to the prepared baking sheet and immediately season lightly with salt.
4. Arrange the pork belly and citrus on a large plate. Sprinkle with the jalapeño and herbs, and douse with the vinaigrette. Use a Microplane to finely grate the peppercorns evenly over the salad. Serve right away.

BRAISED PORK BELLY

MAKES 2 POUNDS BRAISED PORK AND 6½ CUPS FLAVORFUL LIQUID

BRINING THE BELLY

16 cups water
1¾ cups plus **2½** tablespoons kosher salt
¾ cup plus **1** tablespoon granulated sugar
¼ cup black peppercorns, finely ground
1 (3-pound) piece pork belly

COOKING THE BELLY

1 medium yellow onion, coarsely chopped
5 medium garlic cloves, lightly crushed
2 scallions, trimmed and cut into several pieces
3 thyme sprigs
1 large rosemary sprig

Brine the belly

1. In a large mixing bowl, combine the water, salt, sugar, and pepper and stir until the salt and sugar dissolve.
2. Put the belly fat-side down in a baking dish just large enough to hold it snugly. Pour in the brine to completely submerge the pork, cover, and refrigerate for 3 days.

Braise the belly

3. Preheat the oven to 375°F. Cut a piece of parchment paper just large enough to fit inside a large Dutch oven and set aside. Drain the pork belly well and discard the brine. Place the belly fat-side down in the Dutch oven. Add the onion, garlic, scallions, thyme, rosemary, and just enough water to cover. Bring the water to a boil over high heat, cover the belly with the parchment paper, then cover the pot tightly with foil.

4. Transfer to the oven and cook until the belly is very tender (when you flip the belly over and carefully and gently poke the fat, it should give way like custard), about 2½ hours. Remove the pot from the oven, take off the foil and let the pork belly rest in the liquid for 2 hours.

Press the belly

5. Carefully transfer the belly fat-side down to a 9 x 13-inch parchment paper–lined baking sheet. Cover the belly with another piece of parchment paper and put another 9 x 13-inch baking sheet on top so the bottom is touching the belly. Top the tray with about 8 pounds of weight (a gallon jug of water or several large cans of beans will do the trick).
6. Strain the cooking liquid through a fine-mesh sieve into an airtight container. Refrigerate the weighted belly and the cooking liquid in the fridge overnight.
7. The next day, skim the fat from the cooking liquid and reserve for another purpose, or discard. Wrap the belly in plastic wrap and store it and the cooking liquid in the fridge for up to 3 days or in the freezer for up to 3 months.

FISH SAUCE VINAIGRETTE

MAKES ABOUT 1 CUP

¼ cup plus **2** tablespoons freshly squeezed lime juice
¼ cup plus **2** tablespoons water
¼ cup Red Boat Fish Sauce
1½ teaspoons granulated sugar
½-inch knob ginger, finely grated on a Microplane
1 small garlic clove, finely grated on a Microplane
¼ cup grapeseed oil

1. In a medium mixing bowl, combine the lime juice, water, fish sauce, sugar, ginger, and garlic and whisk until the sugar dissolves. Whisk in the oil in a slow stream until well combined.
2. The vinaigrette keeps for up to one week in an airtight container in your refrigerator. Whisk again before serving.

CHAPTER 4

KHO (BRAISES)

ON KHO (BRAISES)

I know I'm not the only one whose mind goes back to childhood after catching a whiff of kho simmering on the stove. One of the dishes that instantly reminds me of my mother is thịt kho, or pork belly braised in a mahogany-hued caramel that's been seasoned with fish sauce, then served simply with steamed rice and a side of vegetables.

Kho is a hallmark of Vietnamese home cooking, made by all Vietnamese households regardless of class. In fact, it was often a telling marker of class: When sugar was expensive, for example, only a monied household could cook up a distinctively sweet kho. A family with less means might have made a kho that was more fish sauce–forward. And during times when meat was very expensive, especially after the war, families made kho quẹt from scraps and reduced the sauce until it was quite thick and intense to stretch it across many bowls of rice. Things have changed since then: Nowadays, kho quẹt is served at fashionable restaurants in Sài Gòn with generous portions of meat and dried shrimp—a testament to the dynamic nature of kho.

At many Vietnamese restaurants, kho, often listed on the menu as "clay pot rice," after the vessel it's sometimes cooked or presented in, is somewhat eclipsed by the popularity of phở and bánh mì, even though most Vietnamese families make kho far, far more often than they make phở or bánh mì. At home, kho is made in large batches and leftovers (there are always leftovers) are stored in casserole dishes for hungry stomachs to

tuck into for the rest of the week. And as much as it is a dish for any day of the week, it is also one you have to make to celebrate the holidays: No Lunar New Year celebration is complete without kho.

Because kho is its own category of Vietnamese cuisine, and is so central to Vietnamese home cooking, we wanted to give it the spotlight it deserves. This chapter is all about the everyday kho we make and its many iterations (see page 229 for the extra-special version we make during the holidays). "Kho" has two meanings in Vietnamese cooking. Very generally, it means any dish that has been braised—as in bò kho, or beef stew—but it also specifically refers to a technique of caramelizing sugar for the braising liquid. This technique, and different ways to use it for different proteins and vegetables, is what we're highlighting in this chapter.

All of our kho recipes start with the same basic first step: caramelizing sugar. This caramelized sugar is the foundation for the braise, and it doesn't take very long to do—in fact, it's very easy for it to cross the threshold from caramelized to burnt, so keep a steady eye on the pot.

Every Vietnamese cook has their own preference when it comes to how much to caramelize the sugar. If we use granulated sugar, we take it a few shades short of burnt. More often than not, we use our palm sugar (see page 251 for more about Red Boat Palm Sugar). The cooking process intensifies its caramel notes, resulting in a deeply flavorful, nutty, multilayered kho.

After the sugar caramelizes, fish sauce and a protein or vegetable is added to braise. Our recipes include a range of bases, including the classic pork belly, shrimp, and chicken kho. Use these recipes as a start, and when you master the basic techniques, explore making kho with different cuts of chicken and pork, or adding other proteins like salmon and tempeh. You can, after all, kho most anything you want.

MONDAY THỊT KHO TIÊU (BRAISED BLACK PEPPER PORK)

We make two types of kho with pork: For the holidays, we make an extra-special version that requires a long 1½- to 2-hour simmer to cook, but when it's ready and plated, its luxuriousness matches the spirit of the feast (see page 229). On other days of the year, we make this thịt kho tiêu. The pork is sliced thin so it'll cook through more quickly, and while you can use either skin-on or skinless pork belly, we opt for skinless pork belly here to further reduce its cooking time. Seasoned generously with black pepper and fragrant with garlic and shallots, this kho is easily one of our family favorites. We make it so often, in fact, that if you peek into our refrigerator at any given time, there's a good chance you'll find a Pyrex casserole dish half-full of this kho, maybe with a spoon still in the dish, glistening with sauce. Thịt kho spooned over fluffy rice, by the way, makes for a fine midnight snack.

SERVES 4

2 pounds pork belly
¼ teaspoon Red Boat Salt or kosher salt
½ tablespoon ground black pepper
1 tablespoon grapeseed, canola, vegetable, or other neutral oil
¼ cup Red Boat Palm Sugar or granulated sugar
⅓ cup minced shallots
3 garlic cloves, minced
3 Thai chiles, split lengthwise, seeds and ribs removed if desired
3 tablespoons Red Boat Fish Sauce

1. Cut the pork belly into 2-inch slabs, then cut the slabs into ½-inch-thick pieces. Season with the salt and pepper. Set aside.
2. In a medium saucepot, combine the oil and sugar. Cook over medium heat, stirring continuously, until the sugar turns a deep amber brown, about 5 minutes.
3. Add the minced shallots and garlic. Sauté over medium heat until aromatic, about 1 minute.
4. Add the pork belly to the pot and stir to coat the pork in the sauce. Cook until the exterior of the pork is no longer pink, 4 to 5 minutes.
5. Add the Thai chiles and Red Boat Fish Sauce. Stir to coat the pork. Cover, lower the heat to low, and simmer until the pork is cooked through and tender, 15 to 25 minutes. Stir every so often to evenly coat the pork.
6. Take the pot off the heat and let the pork steep in the braising liquid for 5 minutes before serving.

GÀ KHO GỪNG (BRAISED GINGER CHICKEN)

This kho, with chicken and plenty of ginger, is one of our family staples. We prefer to use bone-in thighs, as the dark meat is more flavorful than white, and the bone helps keep the meat juicy as it braises in the caramel sauce. To prepare the chicken, we chop the thighs directly across the bone, which is most easily accomplished with a heavy cleaver and a firm, confident grip. If you prefer, you can find similarly chopped chicken prepackaged in the meat section of many Asian markets. Because this is a family favorite, we often make a big pot so everyone can have seconds, or even thirds; the big batch also means we have enough leftovers to pack up for lunch the following day. Whether for lunch or dinner, be sure to have a platter of sliced cucumbers and tomatoes on the table to help cut the richness of the kho.

SERVES 6 TO 8

4 pounds bone-in chicken thighs
½ teaspoon Red Boat Salt or kosher salt
½ tablespoon ground black pepper
¼ cup Red Boat Palm Sugar or granulated sugar
2 tablespoons olive oil
½ cup thinly sliced ginger
1 tablespoon Red Boat Fish Sauce
1 to **3** Thai chiles, seeds and ribs removed if desired (optional)

FOR SERVING

2 to **3** cucumbers, sliced
2 to **3** tomatoes, sliced

1. Cut the chicken thighs across the bone into 2-inch pieces and place in a mixing bowl. Add the salt and pepper, toss to coat the chicken pieces, and set aside.
2. In a pan over medium heat, combine the sugar and oil. Cook the sugar until it's caramelized, stirring constantly to make sure it doesn't burn. You know it is ready when it turns a deep amber brown, 4 to 5 minutes.
3. Add the chopped chicken to the pan. Stir the chicken until all the pieces are coated in the caramelized sauce, about 5 minutes.
4. Add the ginger and cook until the chicken firms up, 15 to 20 minutes. During this process, flip and rotate the chicken every 5 minutes to evenly coat and color the pieces.
5. Once the chicken is firm, add the fish sauce and as few or as many Thai chiles as you'd like. Lower the heat, cover, and simmer until the chicken is tender, about 5 minutes, then remove from the heat. Let the chicken steep in the braising liquid for 5 minutes before serving with the cucumbers and tomatoes.

CÁ KHO (BRAISED CATFISH)

Catfish kho is beloved in so many Vietnamese and Vietnamese American households, and it is definitely a favorite in ours. With its firm, meaty flesh, catfish is an ideal fish to braise. It's also ideal because it's such a quick braise: It needs less than 20 minutes to simmer in the kho before it's ready to serve. While it will be terrific after that short simmer, its flavor will only improve after a night in the refrigerator, when the braising liquid will have completely permeated the catfish. Pair this braise with Pickled Cabbage (page 264), Broccolini with Very Delicious Garlic Sauce (page 76), and, of course, plenty of steamed rice.

SERVES 4 TO 6

1 bunch scallions
2 pounds catfish, cleaned (see page 115) and cut into 1-inch-thick steaks
¼ teaspoon Red Boat Salt or kosher salt
½ teaspoon ground black pepper
1 tablespoon grapeseed, canola, vegetable, or other neutral oil
¼ cup Red Boat Palm Sugar or granulated sugar
3 tablespoons minced garlic
2 to **4** Thai chiles, divided
2 tablespoons Red Boat Fish Sauce

1. Slice the white parts of the scallions into 1-inch segments, then smash the segments with the back of your knife. Slice the green tops into ¼-inch segments. Set both aside.
2. Place the catfish in a mixing bowl and season with the salt and pepper. Toss to coat.
3. In a large pan over medium heat, combine the oil and sugar. Cook the sugar until it's caramelized, stirring constantly to make sure the sugar doesn't burn. The sugar is ready when it turns a deep amber brown, about 5 minutes.
4. Add the whites of the scallions, garlic, and 2 whole Thai chiles to the pan. Sauté until fragrant, about 1 minute.
5. Add the catfish to the pan. Quickly flip the steaks a few times to coat them in the sauce. Add the fish sauce and ¼ cup water.
6. Bring the pan to a boil, then lower the heat to a simmer. Cook for 3 minutes, then gently flip the catfish. As the fish cooks, it will become more delicate and break easily, so be careful. Cover and continue simmering for 10 minutes. Taste. If more heat is desired, add 1 or 2 additional chiles.
7. Take the pan off the heat and garnish the kho with the scallion tops. Let the catfish steep in the braising liquid for 5 minutes before serving.

TÔM KHO TÀU (BRAISED SHRIMP)

Back when the kids were still kids, Ann made this kho at least once or twice a month. The reason she made it so often was because it comes together in less than half an hour—it's that easy and that fast. The critical ingredient here is head-on shrimp. Although they may take a little bit of effort to find depending on where you live, it'll be worth the time to seek them out. The heads contain a pumpkin-orange, buttery paste called tomalley (or roe), and it's that paste that is key to the deep, briny flavor of the dish. You can remove the tails prior to cooking, but, for aesthetic reasons, we prefer to present the dish at the table with them still on.

SERVES 4

⅓ cup kosher salt
2 pounds medium (26/30) head-on shrimp
2 tablespoons olive oil
2 tablespoons minced garlic
2 teaspoons Red Boat Fish Sauce
½ teaspoon ground black pepper
¼ teaspoon granulated sugar
2 scallions, cut into 1-inch pieces
Steamed rice, for serving

1. In a medium mixing bowl, dissolve the salt in 2 quarts of water. Add the shrimp and let it sit in the brine for 15 minutes, then drain and rinse. Gently twist off the shrimps' heads, scoop out the tasty orange tomalley, and set it aside. Peel and devein the shrimp.
2. Pour the oil into a medium-size frying pan over medium heat. Add the garlic and cook, stirring frequently so it doesn't burn.
3. When the garlic becomes aromatic and starts to lightly brown, add the shrimp, tomalley, fish sauce, black pepper, and sugar. Stir constantly until the shrimp is cooked through, 3 to 5 minutes. Remove the pan from the heat.
4. Garnish the shrimp with the scallions and serve with rice.

KHO QUẸT WITH CABBAGE

Kho quẹt is a dish born out of hard times, when protein was scarce in Việt Nam, especially in the countryside. Unlike other kho, where ample pieces of pork, chicken, seafood, or tofu luxuriate in a bath of caramel sauce, kho quẹt relies on a considerably smaller amount of pork and a helping of dried shrimp. The caramel sauce is reduced considerably and thickened, and the flavor becomes intensely concentrated, so much so that some consider this kho more of a dip than a sauce. However you use it, it is an ingenious way to enjoy the beloved kho while on a shoestring budget. Việt Nam's economy has improved since the 1970s, thankfully, and kho quẹt has become a new classic in the Vietnamese culinary canon, to be enjoyed when times are flush or lean. Cabbage is often paired with kho quẹt, and we do so as well here.

SERVES 4

KHO

2 tablespoons dried shrimp

½ cup hot water

2 pounds pork belly, preferably skin-on, diced into ½-inch-wide matchsticks

1 cup finely minced shallots

½ cup finely minced garlic

¼ cup Red Boat Palm Sugar or granulated sugar

¼ cup Red Boat Fish Sauce

3 Thai chiles, seeds and ribs removed if desired, minced

1 teaspoon ground black pepper

CABBAGE

2 tablespoons minced ginger

1 teaspoon kosher salt

1 small cabbage

FOR SERVING

Steamed rice

Make the kho quẹt

1. Soak the dried shrimp in the hot water for 10 minutes, then drain and mince. Set aside until needed.
2. Heat a heavy-bottomed pot over high heat until the pot is screaming hot, about 5 minutes. Add the pork belly, cover, and turn the heat down to low. Cook for 15 minutes.
3. After 15 minutes, uncover the pot and stir the pork to release any pieces that are stuck to the bottom. With a slotted spoon, transfer the pork to a mixing bowl, leaving only the rendered fat in the pot.
4. Add the shallots and garlic to the pot. Gently sauté over low heat until toasted and aromatic, about 5 minutes.
5. Add the sugar, fish sauce, minced dried shrimp, minced chiles, black pepper, and ½ cup of water. Raise the heat to medium and cook for 10 minutes, until the mixture turns a deep caramel color.
6. Return the pork belly to the pot. Add another ½ cup water. Stir to combine.
7. Bring the pot to a boil, then cover and reduce the heat to low. Braise the pork until the liquid reduces and thickens enough to coat the back of a spoon, about 15 minutes.

Boil the cabbage and serve

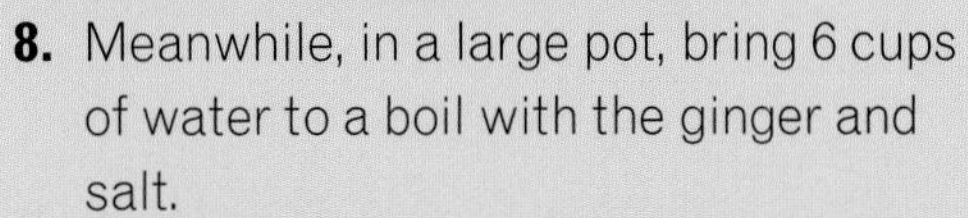

8. Meanwhile, in a large pot, bring 6 cups of water to a boil with the ginger and salt.
9. While the water comes to a boil, cut the cabbage into six wedges. Remove most of the core, leaving just enough to hold the leaves together on each wedge.
10. When the water begins to boil, add half the cabbage. Boil for 5 minutes, then remove from the water and transfer to a serving platter. Repeat with the other half of the cabbage.
11. To serve, spoon the kho quẹt into a large bowl and place on the table with the cabbage. Fill each guest's bowl with steamed rice and dig in, family style.

CHAPTER 5

SEA FOOD

BÚN RIÊU (CRAB NOODLE SOUP)

Bún riêu is a gem somewhat overshadowed by the popularity of phở here, but in Việt Nam, this savory crab noodle soup is much beloved throughout the country. Bún riêu specialists line the streets of busy cities like Sài Gòn, dipping worn paddles into steamy cauldrons with tomatoes and rafts of pork and shellfish—the riêu—bobbling on the surface of a sunset orange broth. Bún riêu has many iterations and every seasoned specialist has their own signature. Older recipes start the broth by crushing tiny whole crabs and filtering out the shells, leaving only the crab meat behind. But because that process is so laborious, and because it's not always easy to find fresh, high-quality crab, ingenious cooks have since come up with other ways to approximate the soup's briny flavor. To make the stock, it's common to use mắm tôm, a fermented shrimp paste found in Asian markets, but we often swap it out in favor of our Red Boat Mắm Nêm, a fermented anchovy paste. To make the riêu, we either make our own crab paste or we pick up a jar of minced prawns in chile and other spices (preferably, the Pro Kwan brand) at the Asian market. This soup is a big hit in our house. It'll be in yours, too.

→ *continued*

SERVES 6 TO 8

STOCK

1¼ pounds pork spareribs
2 tablespoons Red Boat Fish Sauce
1 tablespoon Red Boat Mắm Nêm or mắm tôm (shrimp paste, see page 21)
2 teaspoons granulated sugar
1 pound yellow onions, sliced
1 tablespoon vinegar (optional)

RIÊU

½ cup dried shrimp
3 tablespoons Annatto Oil (page 287), divided
1 small shallot, minced
¼ pound lean ground pork
4 eggs, beaten
½ cup Minced Soft-Shell Crab Paste (page 110) or one 8-ounce jar minced prawns in spices

FILLINGS

1 pound firm tofu, drained for 1 to 2 hours and patted dry with a paper towel
Kosher salt
2 tablespoons vegetable oil
6 large tomatoes, sliced into 1-inch wedges
18 to **24** ounces dried rice vermicelli noodles (approximately 3 ounces per person)

FOR SERVING

1 small banana blossom, thinly sliced
1 small red cabbage, thinly sliced
1 bunch scallions, thinly sliced
2 bunches Vietnamese perilla, finely sliced
1 bunch cilantro, chopped
2 limes, sliced into wedges
Bean sprouts
Mắm tôm (shrimp paste, see page 21) (optional)

Start the stock

1. Heat 2 cups of water in a large pot set over high heat. When the water comes to a boil, add the spareribs and return the water back to a boil. When foam begins to surface, boil for just 1 minute longer, then drain the pork in a colander. Rinse the pork with cold water, taking care to scrub away any impurities clinging to the pork.
2. Clean the pot, then return the spareribs with 2½ quarts of water. Bring the water to a boil, then lower the heat and simmer while you make the riêu.

Make the riêu

3. Place the dried shrimp in a small bowl and cover with hot water. Soak the shrimp until they crumble between your fingers, about 10 minutes. Drain the shrimp and set aside.

4. Heat 1½ tablespoons of the annatto oil to a small pan along with the minced shallot. Fry the shallot over medium heat until it becomes aromatic, about 1 minute. Turn off the heat and set the pan aside to cool.
5. Place the rehydrated shrimp in the bowl of a food processor and process to a fine grind, about 2 minutes. Transfer the ground shrimp to a medium bowl and add the ground pork, eggs, minced soft-shell crab paste or minced prawns, and the shallot with its oil. Using a spoon or your hands, mix until all the ingredients are incorporated.
6. Increase the heat under the pot of simmering spareribs from medium to high and gently slide the entire shrimp-pork mixture on top of the broth in one even layer. The riêu will sink at first; once the pot begins to boil, it will begin to float to the surface. At that point, lower the heat and cook the riêu at a bare simmer until it's firm and cooked through, about 15 minutes. Remove the riêu and let cool. Don't worry if the riêu breaks off in several pieces.

Finish the stock and make the fillings

7. Add the fish sauce, mắm nêm or shrimp paste, sugar, and sliced onions to the pork broth and continue simmering until the ribs are tender and start to separate from the bone, about 40 minutes.
8. As the broth simmers, slice the tofu into 2 x 1½-inch slices. Season the sliced tofu with a pinch of salt. In a large sauté pan over medium heat, heat the vegetable oil. When a drop of water sizzles in the oil, add the tofu slices and cook until golden on all sides. Remove the tofu and drain on paper towels.
9. Using the same pan over medium heat, add the remaining 1½ tablespoons annatto oil with the sliced tomatoes. Sauté for 1 minute. Set aside.
10. Once the pork ribs are tender, transfer the tomatoes and their oil to the broth. Simmer for 5 minutes. Taste the broth. If it needs a little bit more acid, add the vinegar. Add the tofu.
11. Boil the noodles in water according to the package's instructions and portion into six to eight serving bowls. Ladle the broth into each bowl, being sure each bowl gets a spare rib or two, tomatoes, tofu, and pieces of the riêu. Serve with a platter of vegetables, herbs, limes, and mắm tôm for the table.

MINCED SOFT-SHELL CRAB PASTE

Many, especially older, recipes for bún riêu call for the meat of tiny whole crabs. It's not easy to answer that call: The crabs are tiny, their shells thick. Cracking enough crabs to make the soup for family and friends is an extraordinarily laborious process—in other words, a true expression of love. But if you're lucky enough to live in an area where soft-shell crabs are available during their short season between spring and summer, you can express your love with those crabs, shell and all, to make this delicious paste. Use it instead of the jar of minced prawn in spices in our recipe for Bún Riêu (page 107); it's also terrific on fried rice and as a spread on toast. Frozen, the paste will keep for at least 12 months.

MAKES 1½ CUPS

- **¾** pound soft-shell crabs, cleaned
- **1** teaspoon annatto seeds
- **¼** pound (1 stick) butter
- **½** pound red onion, minced
- **¼** cup minced garlic
- **¼** cup minced scallions
- **1** to **3** teaspoons Red Boat Fish Sauce

1. Quarter the crabs and, using a blender or an immersion blender, blitz the crabs until they become a minced paste. Set aside.
2. In a 3-quart heavy-bottomed pot, combine the annatto seeds and butter. Over medium-low heat, cook the butter for a few minutes, just until it starts to foam—don't let the solids brown too much. As the butter melts, the annatto seeds will start to pop and leach their color into the butter. Once the butter turns a vibrant vermillion red, use a slotted spoon or a fine-mesh sieve to remove the annatto seeds. If you use a sieve, pour the strained butter back into the pot.
3. Increase the heat to medium-high and add the red onion, garlic, and scallions to the pot. Sauté until aromatic, just a few minutes.
4. Add the minced crab and 1 teaspoon of fish sauce to the pot. Bring to a boil, then turn down the heat to low.
5. Gently simmer for 45 minutes, stirring often to prevent scorching at the bottom of the pot. Taste and add an additional teaspoon or two of fish sauce if desired. It's ready to use right away, or the paste can be divided into ½-cup portions and frozen for up to 12 months.

CANH CHUA (PINEAPPLE CATFISH SOUP)

If it was on the menu, canh chua was the one dish I always ordered when my mom and I went out to eat back when we were still in Việt Nam. Canh chua originated in the Mekong Delta; its literal translation in English is "sour soup," which is slightly misleading. While the broth does have a distinct acidity thanks to tamarind and tomatoes, there's a lovely sweetness there, too, which comes from the addition of pineapple. Fish sauce, meanwhile, provides a crucial savory boost. Rounding out the bowl are okra, herbs, and Tracy's favorite: slices from the stalk of the elephant ear, a plant in the taro family with enormous leaves. You can find the thick green stems, often labeled under their Vietnamese name, bạc hà, at some Asian and most Southeast Asian markets. Thanks to all these components, the soup is remarkably well balanced—so much so, in fact, that omitting any ingredient will make a noticeable difference. As for the filling, we, like so many other Vietnamese families, use catfish, though we've also successfully subbed in salmon in a pinch. Canh chua now is a family staple, a dish we make often at home to start a meal or as part of a wide spread of dishes.

→ *continued*

SERVES 4 TO 6

½ cup seedless tamarind paste (see page 25)
3 tablespoons olive oil
⅓ cup minced garlic
2 Thai chiles or jalapeños, seeds and ribs removed if desired, sliced
1 tablespoon granulated sugar
2 to **3** tablespoons Red Boat Fish Sauce
1 pound whole catfish, cut into steaks and cleaned (see Note, opposite)
1½ cups chopped pineapple, preferably fresh
1 bạc hà (giant elephant ear stalk), peeled and cut on the bias into ¼-inch-thick slices
¾ pound Roma tomatoes, quartered, or cherry tomatoes, halved
7 okra pods, cut on the bias into ¼-inch-thick slices

FOR SERVING

½ cup chopped ngò gai (sawtooth coriander)
1 cup coarsely chopped ngổ ôm (rice paddy herb)
½ cup chopped Thai basil
2 cups bean sprouts
1 Thai chile, thinly sliced

1. Place the tamarind paste in a bowl and cover with boiling water. Using the back of a spoon, gently mash the paste against the bowl and stir until the paste breaks down in the water. Strain the tamarind to remove the pulp and set aside the tamarind juice.
2. Place a large pot over medium heat and pour in the olive oil. When it starts to smoke, add the minced garlic and turn the heat to low. Fry the garlic, stirring constantly to prevent burning. When the garlic turns golden, use a strainer to transfer half of the fried garlic to a bowl.
3. Add 1⅓ cups of water to the pot with the remaining garlic, along with the chiles. Bring the water to a boil, add 1 cup of the tamarind juice, sugar, and fish sauce. Reduce the heat to a simmer.
4. Add the catfish and pineapple to the pot. Simmer for 10 minutes, then remove the catfish and set aside while you finish the soup.
5. Add the elephant ear, tomatoes, and okra. Simmer until the elephant ear becomes tender, about 5 minutes. Remove from heat.
6. To serve, place a piece of catfish in each serving bowl, and divide the soup among the bowls. Serve immediately, alongside a plate of herbs, bean sprouts, and chiles, and the bowl of fried garlic for guests to garnish as they wish.

As with most ingredients, the fresher the fish, the better. If possible, head to an Asian market, where you'll find the elephant ear and herbs for this recipe. You'll also have your pick of live catfish swimming in one of the holding tanks. Note that catfish often have a viscous substance on their skin that should be removed before cooking. Local fishmongers and counters sometimes will remove it for you; if not, ask the fishmonger to gut and chop the fish into 1-inch steaks.

Then, once in your kitchen, rinse the catfish and use the sharp side of a knife to scrape and loosen any remaining viscera clinging to the bones. Sprinkle the catfish with kosher salt, then use the back of the knife to scrape the gelatinous liquid off the skin. Rinse the fish and run your thumb along the skin. If any of the slime is still there, apply more salt to the skin and repeat. When it has all been removed, place the fish in a mixing bowl. Add ½ cup white vinegar and gently stir to coat the steaks with the vinegar. Set the bowl aside for 10 minutes, then drain. Rinse the fish and blot dry with paper towels. It's now ready for cooking.

CHẠO TÔM (SUGARCANE SHRIMP)

My sister's place has long been the spot where the entire Phamily would come together to catch up, especially during the summers when the kids were out on vacation and the daylight stretched long into the evening. Cooking and eating, of course, were a huge part of these gatherings, and the grill stayed hot throughout it all, sizzling with skewers of Nem Nướng (page 149), or these bundles of chạo tôm, shrimp freshly ground into a savory paste and wrapped around sweet sugarcane stalks. If you are fortunate enough to have a local farmer with fresh sugarcane at your neighborhood farmers market, pick up a few stalks and make good use of them in this recipe. Otherwise, canned sugarcane is widely available at Asian grocers and will work just fine. The chạo tôm are great snacks to nosh on, especially when dunked right into our special Peanut-Coconut Nước Chấm. You can also slide the shrimp into moistened rice paper wrappers, or serve them as part of a rice noodle bowl.

MAKES ABOUT 20 SUGARCANE SHRIMP

1¼ pounds shrimp, peeled, deveined, and patted dry

2 scallions, white root ends only

¼ cup minced garlic

2 tablespoons toasted rice powder (see page 23)

2 tablespoons minced shallots

2 teaspoons granulated sugar

2 teaspoons Red Boat Fish Sauce

½ tablespoon vegetable oil, plus a small bowl of oil for shaping

½ teaspoon ground white pepper

1 (20-ounce) can sugarcane, drained, quartered, and cut into 4-inch sticks

→ *continued*

FOR SERVING
1 head lettuce
1 bunch mint
1 bunch Thai basil
1 bunch cilantro
Peanut-Coconut Nước Chấm (page 281)
Rice noodles or rice paper wrappers (optional)

1. To the bowl of a food processor, add the shrimp, scallions, garlic, toasted rice powder, shallots, sugar, fish sauce, oil, and white pepper. Pulse for 15 to 20 times, then test if the paste is ready: Take 2 tablespoons of the shrimp paste and form it into a ball. If the paste holds the shape without flattening on the bottom, it's ready. If not, pulse a few more times and re-test, being sure not to overprocess the paste, or it will fall apart and become mealy. Cover the shrimp paste and place in the fridge to firm up for 1 hour.
2. If grilling, place your grate over low coals or preheat the grill to medium. If baking, preheat the oven to 350°F. If cooking on stovetop, oil a cast-iron pan and set it aside.
3. To shape the shrimp paste, first dip your fingers in the bowl of oil and coat your hands to prevent the shrimp paste from sticking to them. Pinch off about 2 tablespoons of the shrimp paste and flatten it in your palm. Place a sugarcane in the middle of the paste and close your palm to wrap the paste around the sugarcane. The shrimp paste should cover most of the sugarcane, leaving just about ½ inch on each end. Pinch the ends of the paste to seal it onto the sugarcane. Apply a coat of oil onto each sugarcane shrimp. Repeat for the remaining shrimp paste.
4. **If grilling:** Grill the shrimp for 10 to 15 minutes, rotating the stalks every 3 minutes to ensure even cooking.
   If baking: Place the shrimp on a baking sheet and bake for 10 minutes, rotating the shrimp and the pan after 5 minutes.
   If cooking on the stovetop: Heat the well-oiled cast-iron skillet over medium and cook the chạo tôm for 8 to 10 minutes, rotating the chạo tôm every 3 minutes.
5. To serve, place the chạo tôm on a serving platter and set on the table along with the lettuce, herbs, peanut-coconut nước chấm for dipping, and, if using, rice noodles or rice wrappers.

BUTTERFLIED GRILLED PERCH

The DNA of this dish is one part Phú Quốc and one part Nayarit by way of Los Angeles. It came about during a recent trip to Phú Quốc, when seeing all the fish sizzling on the grills there brought to mind chef Sergio Peñuelas and pescado zarandeado. A specialty of Nayarit, Mexico, pescado zarandeado involves butterflying a whole fish, lacquering it in a mayonnaise marinade, then grilling it. Peñuelas serves his with a bowl of deeply caramelized onions and warm corn tortillas. Our version takes a similar approach, though we marinate our fish—a whole perch—in a paste of butter, fish sauce, and turmeric. If you've never gutted and deboned a fish, ask your fishmonger to do so for you; otherwise, the perch is small and forgiving enough that you'll have success doing it in your own kitchen (see page 122). In a pinch, fillets, while not as dramatic as a whole fish, will also do just fine.

SERVES 3 TO 4

6 garlic cloves
2 shallots, roughly chopped
1 to **4** Thai chiles, seeds and ribs removed if desired
2 tablespoons Red Boat Palm Sugar or granulated sugar
2 tablespoons Red Boat Fish Sauce
4 teaspoons turmeric powder
8 tablespoons butter, softened and divided
1 red onion, thinly sliced
1 (2-pound) whole perch, scaled, gutted, and deboned

FOR SERVING

1 bunch rau răm
1 bunch mint
1 bunch Thai basil
1 bunch cilantro
All-Purpose Nước Chấm, Điệp Pham's Nước Chấm, or Calamansi Nước Chấm (pages 275, 277, or 279)
1 stack corn tortillas

→ *continued*

1. Preheat your grill.
2. In a food processor, add garlic, shallots, one or more chiles (depending on your spice preference), sugar, fish sauce, turmeric powder, and 4 tablespoons of butter. Process the marinade until it's smooth.
3. Spoon 2 tablespoons of the marinade into a heatproof ramekin or bowl. Add the sliced onions and remaining 4 tablespoons of butter and set aside.
4. Brush the marinade all over the deboned fish, reserving the remaining marinade to baste the fish during grilling. Lay the perch flat inside a grill basket and secure the latch if your basket has one. Marinate the fish at room temperature for 15 minutes.
5. Place both the fish and the bowl of onions over low coals, if using a grill, or over low heat. Grill the fish for a total of 8 to 10 minutes, flipping and reapplying the marinade every 2 minutes, until the fish is golden brown on both sides.
6. Once the fish is cooked through, take the grill basket off the fire. Gently open the basket and transfer the fish to a platter. Take the ramekin of onions and butter off the heat.
7. To serve, place the platter and onions together with the herb plate, nước chấm, and the tortillas on the table.

HOW TO DEBONE FISH

If your fishmonger is unavailable to debone the perch for you, you can do so at home. Begin by inspecting the fish to make sure there are no scales on the skin. Use cooking shears to cut and remove the dorsal and pectoral fins, then cut away the collar and remove the gills from the body of the fish. Discard the gills.

Orient the fish so its head is pointing toward your carving hand. Turn the fish on its side and run your knife down both sides of the spine, all the way from the collar to the base of the tail. Use shears to detach the spine from the head and the tail. Lift the spine up: The sides of the fish should fall away. Use shears to cut the rest of the spine from the flesh. Lay the fish flat, skin-side up. Working from the inside out, remove the rib bones by running your knife between the flesh and bones. Lift the bones away as you carve. Collect the bones in a resealable freezer bag and use them to make Fish Stock (page 296).

ON THE RED BOAT

RED BOAT

CATCHING ANCHOVIES

The waters of Phú Quốc are beautiful. They're crystal clear, glistening with emerald green that gives way to an infinite blue as you drift further from the shore. The temperature and ecosystem of these waters are especially hospitable to all sorts of ocean life, including the precious fish we use to make Red Boat Fish Sauce: cá cơm thang, or black anchovies.

Slender and not much longer than a pinky finger, black anchovies contain uncommonly high levels of glutamates, the protein responsible for the distinctive flavor of umami. These special anchovies are the only ingredient in our fish sauce other than salt. It takes about 5 pounds of anchovies to make one 500 milliliter bottle of Red Boat.

We catch the anchovies year-round, but the height of the fishing season is between the early summer and late fall. Fishing is done at night, and it's a collective effort. Light boats—boats with lighted arms that, from a distance, look like glowing lollipops—motor ahead first, scouting for fish. Ideally, a school of anchovies will soon be attracted to the light, at which point the fishing boats are called in to surround the swarm, drop the nets, and make the catch. The reality, though, is that fishing requires as much patience as the sea is deep. It may take hours for enough fish to swarm.

Once they do, everyone springs into action. When the anchovies are caught, the crew uses pulleys to lift and position the heavy net over the deck, then the catch is released. Our goal is to net only anchovies, but we do end up with some bycatch, which is essentially any fish other than what we intended to catch. Sometimes the bycatch is worth more at the local fish market than the anchovies! But to us, the anchovies are the real prize, so experienced hands and eyes separate any fish that are not anchovies. The bycatch is saved for the crew to sell or take home, and the anchovies are immediately salted. This is critical: Salting sooner rather than later not only preserves the anchovies' flavor, it also kills off any unwanted bacteria on the fish, prevents spoilage, and jump-starts the fermentation process.

Once the anchovies are unloaded, the nets are folded up, the light boats head out in search of another good fishing spot, and the waiting begins anew. When the hulls are full, the boats head in and rendezvous with smaller transfer boats that can better navigate the narrow channels leading back to our barrel house. Those boats dock right outside our barrel house and the crew carries the anchovies from the boats, one basket at a time, and unloads them into the fermentation barrels. While the boats are docked and the crew takes a much-deserved break, torn fishing nets are then taken to local seamstresses nearby, who most often do their work in small groups surrounded by curtains of netting waiting to be mended.

Back at the barrel house, the fermentation process really begins. It takes about one year for the anchovies to break down into a deep amber liquid, scented with the sea, and packed with that distinctive smack of umami.

THE RED BOAT CREW

We are incredibly fortunate to have the fishing crew that we have at Red Boat. Our captain has been with us since around 2013, and many others on the team have been with us for just as long. This long-standing relationship has been crucial to our success.

In the earliest days of making fish sauce, I did what others advised me to do. That is, I bought salted fish from local suppliers, then tossed them into the fermentation barrels. Then, essentially, I crossed my fingers: I could only hope that the final product would have the clarity and purity of flavor I so longed for. Unsurprisingly, this didn't quite work out. Sometimes, the fish I bought had too much bycatch; other times, the fish just weren't salted properly. Each time, none of these issues would be apparent until after the fermentation process was over, some twelve months later. After one less-than-ideal batch too many, I realized that to make the fish sauce I wanted to make, I needed to do more than just cross my fingers. I needed a more direct relationship with a fishing crew who could help me oversee the process from the very start.

From that point on, I've had a dedicated Red Boat fishing crew. It was because of the crew's keen observations and feedback as we cycled through different salts that we were able to build Red Boat into what it is today. Our crew is made of excellent fishermen, their instincts and knowledge honed by their seafaring experience and respect for Ông Trời and his power to bestow good weather and a successful harvest. They know when it's too windy to catch fish, the signs that foretell a coming storm, and where the anchovies may be going based on the direction of the currents. They maintain our quality standards and ensure that the anchovies, once caught, are immediately salted just the right way.

While the arrangement with our fishermen isn't unique, the predominant model to source fish in the fish sauce industry involves middlemen. I've found investing in a direct relationship instead has been critical to better control the quality of our fish sauce and to ensure our fishermen are treated fairly and compensated equitably. Without this great crew, there is no great fish sauce.

SUSTAINABILITY

Anchovies are one of the more sustainable fish in the ocean. They are pretty low on the food chain, remarkably resilient, and quick to adapt. It is nonetheless important to us that we engage in responsible fishing practices: We limit our bycatch, for instance, and use purse seine nets to limit the environmental degradation of the seabed. The netting also is designed with mesh specifically sized to catch only fully mature, rather than young, anchovies.

When I first started making fish sauce, anchovies were plentiful near the shore. Over the last few years, though, commercial development has increased around Phú Quốc's coast, and the anchovies have rerouted in response, finding more hospitable grounds further into the Gulf of Thailand. As we've followed them there, we've continued to be mindful of our environmental responsibility. Being conscientious stewards of the sea is one way, we hope, that we can preserve this centuries-old tradition of making fish sauce for generations to come.

CRAB ROLLS

Depending on where you live, crab season can be year-round or just a few precious months between the fall and early spring. Wherever you are, these crab rolls are a great, easy way to make the most of the season. We like to simply steam the crab to retain as much of its natural flavor as possible—in fact, many supermarket seafood counters and fishmongers will provide steaming services if you ask. From there, the crab is dressed with a mayonnaise amped up with fish sauce, then piled high on buttery split-top or sweet Hawaiian rolls. We can't resist having a warm roll as soon as it's assembled, but the rolls are also delicious cold.

MAKES 6 ROLLS

CRAB

2¼ pounds whole crab
Zest of 1 lemon
3 tablespoons chopped dill fronds
⅛ teaspoon ground black pepper
¼ red onion, minced

DRESSING

1 teaspoon Red Boat Fish Sauce
2 teaspoons lemon juice
1½ teaspoons mustard powder
2 tablespoons mayonnaise, preferably Best Foods

ROLLS

6 split-top rolls or 12 Hawaiian rolls, unseparated
2 tablespoons butter, divided

→ *continued*

Prepare the crab

1. If your fishmonger does not provide steaming services, steam the crab by first filling a steamer with 1½ inches of water. Bring the water to a boil over high heat, then add the crabs, cover, steam for 15 minutes, then remove. Once the crabs have cooled enough to handle, remove the crab meat from the shells. You should end up with about 1½ cups of crab meat, or ½ pound.
2. Place the crab meat in a mixing bowl along with the lemon zest, chopped dill fronds, and black pepper. Set aside.
3. Soak the minced red onion in 3 cups of water for 10 minutes, then drain and add to the crab mixture.
4. In a small bowl, make the dressing by mixing together the fish sauce, lemon juice, mustard powder, and mayonnaise.
5. Pour the dressing over the crab meat mixture. Use a fork to gently incorporate the dressing with the crab. Cover and chill in the refrigerator for at least 20 minutes.

Prepare the buns and assemble the rolls

6. If using Hawaiian rolls, pull apart the rolls a pair at a time, being careful to keep the pair adjoined. A packet of 12 rolls will yield 6 large buns. (Regular split-top rolls are twice as long, so you will only need 6 of those if you use them instead.)
7. Heat a medium skillet over medium heat. Add 1 tablespoon butter to the pan and toast the rolls, adding the additional tablespoon of butter as necessary. Transfer the rolls to a cooling rack.
8. If using Hawaiian rolls, split the top of each pair of buns. To assemble, carefully spoon ¼ cup crab mixture into each roll. Serve immediately.

SEAFOOD CHOWDER

This seafood chowder is for all seasons, whether it's a relaxing end to a lazy summer day, or a much-needed bowl of warmth in the bluster of winter. Our version is loosely based on the classic creamy New England–style chowder, adding a healthy bit of fish sauce to deepen the broth. We also load it up with shrimp and crab; you can use frozen shrimp, but we encourage you to take the time to source fresh crab, as it will make all the difference in flavor. Your local fishmonger or Asian markets are great sources of live crab, and many will even offer steaming services free of charge with your purchase. Take them up on the offer. That will save you an extra step without sacrificing quality.

SERVES 4 TO 6

2 teaspoons baking soda
3 tablespoons kosher salt
1 pound large shrimp, peeled and deveined
3 pounds whole crab, steamed
6 tablespoons butter
Zest from 1 small lemon
1 large onion, minced
1 celery rib, minced
1¾ cups Buttery Shellfish Stock (page 297) or Fish Stock (page 296) (or store-bought)
½ pound white potatoes, diced into 1-inch cubes
1 bay leaf
1 Thai chile, seeds and ribs removed if desired, minced
1 tablespoon Red Boat Fish Sauce
Leaves from 1 sprig fresh thyme
1¾ cups heavy whipping cream
½ cup parsley leaves, minced

→ *continued*

1. In a medium mixing bowl, dissolve the baking soda and salt into 1 quart of water. Add the shrimp and let it sit in the brine in the refrigerator while you prepare the crab.
2. To prepare the crab, start by removing the shells and gills. Discard the gills. Reserve the crab meat and mustard (the yellowish substance next to the meat) in separate bowls and store in the refrigerator until needed.

3. Remove the shrimp from the brine and press between paper towels to dry. Place three-fourths of the shrimp in a bowl and return it to the refrigerator until needed. Roughly chop the remaining shrimp into ½-inch pieces.
4. Melt the butter in a heavy-bottomed stockpot over medium-high heat. Once the butter starts to foam, add the chopped shrimp. Stirring constantly, sauté the shrimp for 1 to 2 minutes, until the shrimp is caramelized.
5. Turn off the heat and use a slotted spoon to transfer the shrimp to a bowl. Spoon 2 tablespoons of the butter from the pot over the shrimp. Add the lemon zest to the shrimp. Toss to combine and store in the refrigerator until ready to serve.
6. Turn the heat back to medium-high and add the onion and celery to the pot. Sauté until browned, about 15 minutes.
7. Add the reserved crab mustard. Sauté for 3 minutes, then add 3 tablespoons water to deglaze the pot, making sure to scrape up any of the flavorful caramelized onion bits at the bottom.
8. Add the stock, potatoes, bay leaf, Thai chile, and fish sauce. Crush the thyme leaves between your hands and add those to the pot, too. Bring the pot to a boil, then lower the heat and simmer until potatoes are easily pierced with a fork, 15 to 20 minutes.
9. Once the potatoes are tender, add the heavy whipping cream and reserved uncooked shrimp. Simmer until the shrimp start to turn pink, then add three-fourths of the crabmeat. Remove the bay leaf.
10. Ladle the chowder into bowls and top with a spoonful each of the remaining crab meat and the sautéed shrimp, plus a good pinch of minced parsley. Serve immediately.

WALNUT PESTO WITH SHRIMP

Pesto is often made with a hard cheese, like Parmigiano-Reggiano or Pecorino Romano, but here we've swapped that umami ingredient for another umami powerhouse: fish sauce. The result is a delicious pesto with a subtle but pronounced savoriness, and it's especially great when you have a hankering for a pesto pasta but don't have the right cheese on hand. We use a mix of basil and parsley as the foundation of the pesto; the combination of the two herbs make for a wonderfully bright sauce that is as green as springtime grass. The parsley also will help keep that color for a few days—and it happens to pair exceptionally well with shrimp.

SERVES 4

3 tablespoons kosher salt
2 teaspoons baking soda
1 pound peeled and deveined shrimp
4 ounces walnuts
3 garlic cloves
2 teaspoons Red Boat Fish Sauce
Ground black pepper
2 cups (3 ounces) basil leaves
1 cup (1 ounce) parsley
1 cup plus **2** tablespoons extra-virgin olive oil, divided
1 pound spaghetti

→ *continued*

1. Place the salt, baking soda, and 1 quart of water in a medium bowl. Stir to dissolve the salt and baking powder. Add the shrimp and leave them in the brine for 15 minutes, then remove. Blot dry with paper towels. Set aside until needed.
2. Place the walnuts in a single layer in a skillet. Over a low flame, toast the walnuts for 5 minutes, shaking the pan constantly to avoid burning them. The walnuts are done when they become fragrant. Transfer the walnuts to a plate and set aside to cool.
3. Once the walnuts are cool enough to handle, roughly chop them and transfer to the bowl of a food processor.
4. Add the garlic, fish sauce, and a pinch of black pepper to the food processor. Pulse the mixture a few times until the walnuts are minced, then add the basil and parsley and pulse two more times.
5. Scrape down the sides of the bowl, then, with the motor running, slowly pour in 1 cup of the olive oil in a thin stream until the oil is well incorporated and emulsified. Transfer the pesto to a bowl. Set aside.
6. Cook and drain the spaghetti according to manufacturer's instructions, reserving 1 cup of the pasta water.
7. Over high heat, add the remaining 2 tablespoons of olive oil to a large skillet. Working in batches as necessary to avoid overcrowding the pan, sear the shrimp for 1 minute on each side.
8. After all the shrimp have been seared, add the pesto and spaghetti. Sauté for 2 minutes, stirring constantly, until the shrimp are just cooked through. If the pasta looks too dry, add reserved pasta water as needed. Serve immediately.

BÚN KÈN (COCONUT FISH WITH NOODLES)

Bún kèn is one of the most delicious bowls of noodles you can find in Phú Quốc. A street food specialty of the Kiên Giang province, the dish takes advantage of the island's abundance of fish and coconut, though its true magic lies in the thoughtful, considered layering of multiple components and textures. Yellowtail collar is the foundation for our stock, which you can source at Japanese and Korean markets, or any market with a strong sashimi program. From there, the stock melds with coconut cream and lemongrass to create a tangy, bright orange curry. The curry is ladled over a spool of warm noodles, then topped with a drizzle of coconut fish sauce and a blanket of fresh herbs—including rau răm, or Vietnamese coriander, which you can omit if you don't have it readily available. A few slices of fresh chile bring the whole bowl together. Making this dish brings back fond memories of Phú Quốc—and also reminds us of the island's proximity to Cambodia: In Khmer cuisine, "kèn" refers to any dish with coconut cream. This recipe is our tribute to the dish.

→ *continued*

SERVES 4 TO 6

STOCK

1 pound yellowtail collar
¼ pound shallots, diced
¼ teaspoon whole black peppercorns
1 stalk lemongrass
1 cup cilantro stems

CURRY SAUCE

⅔ cup Annatto Oil (page 287), divided
½ pound white onion, diced
1 cup finely minced lemongrass (see page 20)
2 ounces cilantro root, or **4** ounces cilantro stems, minced
2 tablespoons minced garlic
3 tablespoons turmeric powder
1½ cups coconut cream
2 tablespoons minced fresh makrut lime leaves, midribs removed
2 to **4** Thai chiles
¼ cup Red Boat Fish Sauce

FOR SERVING AND GARNISH

6 cups cooked vermicelli rice noodles
1 bunch rau răm (see page 20)
2 cups bean sprouts
1 bunch basil leaves
1 bunch cilantro leaves
1½ cups shredded Japanese cucumber
1 cup shredded green papaya (seeds removed and peeled)
½ cup shredded carrot
Coconut Nước Chấm for Bún Kèn (page 144)

Make the stock

1. Place the yellowtail collars in a pot large enough to fit the collars snugly. Add the diced shallots and peppercorns.
2. Trim the lemongrass tops until you see the pink center. Discard the portion of the lemongrass that was above this pink center, leaving only the lemongrass base. Halve the lemongrass lengthwise and use the back of your knife to bruise and smash the base of the lemongrass, then add both halves to the pot.
3. Using the same knife technique, bruise and smash the cilantro stems, then add them to the pot.
4. Add 5 cups water. The water should cover the yellowtail collars. Bring the pot to a boil, then reduce the heat to low and simmer for 20 minutes.
5. Turn off the heat and remove the yellowtail collars from the pot. Once they are cool enough to handle, separate the meat from the bone.
6. Return the bones to the pot. Let the bones steep for another 15 minutes, then line a strainer with a fine mesh cloth and strain the stock into a mixing bowl. Discard the solids.
7. Rinse the pot to remove any remaining grit, then return the stock to the pot. Return the meat from the fish to the pot and put it all aside while you make the curry sauce.

Build the curry sauce

8. In a medium pan over medium-high heat, add 3 tablespoons of annatto oil and the diced white onion. Resist the urge to stir the onions: let them fry undisturbed until slightly charred, about 5 minutes. Transfer the oil and onions to the fish stock, then pour ¼ cup of the stock into the pan to deglaze it, using a silicone spatula to scrape the pan clean.
9. Lower the heat to medium and add the remaining (a generous ⅓ cup) annatto oil, the minced lemongrass, cilantro roots, and garlic. Stirring constantly, toast until fragrant, about 5 minutes. Add the turmeric powder and cook for 15 seconds, then transfer the whole mixture to the fish stock.
10. Using the same saucepan, add the coconut cream, makrut lime leaves, and chiles and turn the heat up to high. Use your spatula to dislodge any bits of lemongrass, cilantro, or garlic that have stuck to the bottom of the pan. Once the cream starts to boil, turn off the heat and let the leaves and chiles steep for 10 minutes.
11. Pour the coconut cream, leaves, and chiles into fish stock, and add the fish sauce as well. Stir to combine and set aside.

Assemble the bún kèn

12. Cook the noodles according to the instructions on the package. For each serving, place 1 cup of the cooked noodles at the bottom of a serving bowl.
13. Place a few pinches of each garnish atop the noodles, then spoon 1 tablespoon of the Coconut Nước Chấm over the noodles.
14. If the curry sauce has cooled, reheat it by bringing it to a gentle boil, then spoon a few ladlefuls over the noodles.
15. Serve the bowls of bún kèn alongside a platter of any remaining garnishing herbs, as well as the Coconut Nước Chấm for guests to further customize their bowl, if desired.

When you order bún kèn to go in Phú Quốc, each component of the dish is packaged separately so you can build your own fresh bowl at home. If you have leftovers here, do as the vendors do on the island and store the noodles, curry sauce, and nước chấm in their own individual containers and reassemble as needed.

COCONUT NƯỚC CHẤM FOR BÚN KÈN

The nước chấm we use throughout this book can be paired with a variety of dishes—well, all except one. This coconut nước chấm is specifically intended for use in our Bún Kèn (page 140). On its own, it is concentrated, intense, and sweet. Once diluted with the other components in the bún kèn, however, it opens up and blossoms, bringing all the flavors together in the bowl.

MAKES ABOUT 2 CUPS

¼ cup Red Boat Fish Sauce
2 Thai chiles, seeds and ribs removed if desired, minced
2 garlic cloves, minced
1 teaspoon apple cider vinegar or lime juice
1 cup Red Boat Palm Sugar or granulated sugar
7 ounces coconut water

1. In a small pot, bring all the ingredients to a boil.
2. Remove from the heat and let the nước chấm cool before transferring into a jar. It's ready to use immediately. It will keep in the refrigerator, covered, for up to 1 week.

CHAPTER 6

PORK

NEM NƯỚNG (GRILLED PORK MEATBALLS)

Even with as much cooking as my mother did when I was growing up, we only had nem nướng in restaurants and street stalls. That's because after they're shaped into meatballs, they're skewered and cooked on a searing hot grill—which my family did not have in Việt Nam. Once we moved to the United States, though, that changed: We got ourselves a backyard grill, and it was suddenly possible to make nem nướng at home. In fact, those springy meatballs became a big part of our Sundays, when everyone, including my mom and our extended family, would meet up at my sister's house to catch up and, of course, to cook and eat. We got pretty good at making the meatballs: Tracy, Tiffany, and their cousins rolled the meatballs. My mom and sister were on QC, checking that the meatballs were the same size and shape so they'd all cook evenly when handed off to my brother at the grill station. This is when my mom's sense of humor would come out: If someone's meatball was too large, she'd rib them with, "Who do you plan to feed with this?" All this is to say that making these springy meatballs to eat with bún (rice noodles) or rice paper wrappers and a plate of herbs is a great way to spend time with family and friends. This recipe feeds the entire Phamily, but it can be easily halved for a smaller party. And while we grill the meatballs here, you also can cook them in a hot pan on the stove. They won't have the smokey flavor from a grill, but they'll be delicious all the same.

→ *continued*

Mixing ground pork for nem nướng (meatballs)

MAKES 30 TO 35 MEATBALLS

3⅓ pounds pork belly, skin removed
½ cup packed brown sugar
¼ cup minced fresh garlic
2 tablespoons plus **1** teaspoon Red Boat Salt or kosher salt
1 tablespoon white wine
1 tablespoon vegetable oil
Wooden skewers, soaked in water for at least 30 minutes

FOR SERVING

Rice paper wrappers or bún (rice noodles)
Lettuce
1 bunch rau răm
1 bunch mint
1 bunch Thai basil
1 bunch cilantro
Red Boat Salt-Pickled Daikon and Carrots (page 265)
All-Purpose Nước Chấm, Điệp Pham's Nước Chấm, or Peanut-Coconut Nước Chấm (pages 275, 277, and 281)

1. Slice the belly into large pieces and place in the bowl of a food processor. Process the pork to a fine grind, then transfer to a large bowl. Add the brown sugar, garlic, salt, and white wine. Using your hands or a wooden spoon, mix everything until well combined.
2. Cover the bowl with plastic wrap and refrigerate for at least 2 hours, preferably overnight.
3. Remove the pork from the fridge. Scoop out generous spoonfuls of pork and shape into meatballs about the size of a golf ball. If you're grilling, thread the meatballs onto the skewers. With the palm of your hand, gently flatten the meatballs into thick patties.
4. **If grilling:** Use the oil to oil the grates and preheat the grill to medium heat or 350°F. Grill the skewered nem nướng, flipping occasionally, until both sides are golden brown and the meat is firm and cooked through, 10 to 20 minutes total.
   If cooking on the stove top: Place a large sauté pan over medium heat and add the vegetable oil. When the oil shimmers, add the nem nướng, working in batches as necessary to avoid crowding the pan. Cook the patties until they're golden brown, firm, and cooked through, about 5 minutes per side.
5. To serve, arrange the nem nướng on serving platters and place them on the table, along with the rice paper wrappers or rice noodles, lettuce, herbs, pickles, and nước chấm.

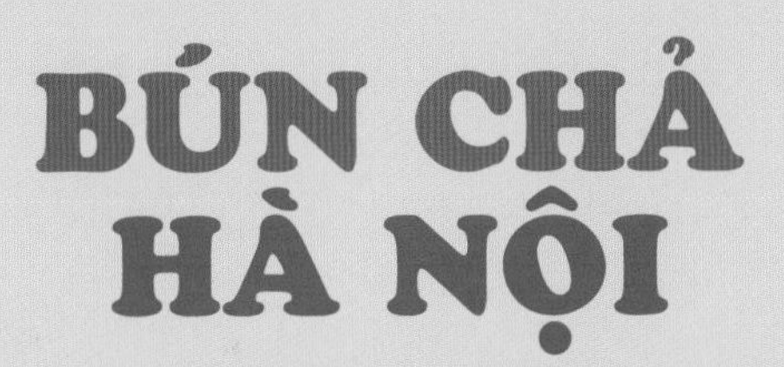

BÚN CHẢ HÀ NỘI

(NOODLE SALAD WITH PORK PATTIES)

For a long while, you were more likely to encounter the southern Vietnamese dish of bún thịt nướng than its northern counterpart, bún chả, in Vietnamese restaurants stateside. That changed in 2016, when President Barack Obama shared a bowl of bún chả with Anthony Bourdain at Bún Chả Hương Liên in Hà Nội, and, well, the rest is noodle history: Their table is now preserved under glass at the restaurant, and bún chả enjoys a newfound popularity in America (in fact, we've seen it listed as an "Obama bowl" on a few Vietnamese restaurant menus here!). Unlike bún thịt nướng, where grilled pork sits atop rice noodles with a small bowl of nước chấm on the side, bún chả separates the meat from the noodles, placing all the pork, including the chả (pork patties), in the nước chấm itself. To make the chả, we use a combination of shoulder and belly. To achieve the coarse texture ideal for forming the patties, grind the pork yourself in your food processor, or ask your butcher to run the meat through the grinder just once.

SERVES 4 TO 6

MARINADE

- **¼** pound scallions, chopped into 1-inch lengths
- **1** shallot, roughly chopped
- **6** cloves garlic, roughly chopped
- **3** tablespoons Red Boat Fish Sauce
- **2** tablespoons grapeseed, canola, vegetable, or other neutral oil
- **1** tablespoon plus **1** teaspoon granulated sugar
- **1** teaspoon ground black pepper

→ *continued*

1¼ pounds pork belly, skin removed, sliced ¼ inch thick
1 pound ground pork shoulder
¼ pound ground pork belly, skin removed
Wooden skewers, soaked in water for 30 minutes

FOR SERVING
1 head butter lettuce
1 bunch mint
1 bunch cilantro
6 cups cooked rice vermicelli noodles
1 cup toasted peanuts, chopped (optional)
Fried Shallots (page 290) (optional)
All-Purpose Nước Chấm or Điệp Pham's Nước Chấm (page 275 and 277)
Red Boat Salt–Pickled Daikon and Carrots (page 265)

Marinate the pork

1. Combine the scallions, shallot, garlic, fish sauce, oil, sugar, and black pepper in the small bowl of a food processor. Process into a smooth paste, then divide the marinade between two mixing bowls.
2. In one bowl of marinade, add the sliced pork belly. Mix well to incorporate the marinade into the meat, then marinate in the refrigerator for at least 2 hours and up to 24 hours.
3. In the other bowl of marinade, add the ground shoulder and ground belly. Knead the mixture to incorporate the marinade into the meat, then form patties by scooping about 2 tablespoons of the mixture and rolling it into a 1-inch meatball. Place the meatball on a baking sheet and repeat with the remaining mixture, spacing the meatballs 2 inches apart. Chill for at least 2 hours and up to 24 hours, to firm up.

Grill the pork and serve

4. Preheat the grill to 350°F.
5. Thread the sliced pork belly onto skewers and use the tines of a fork to flatten the meatballs into 2-inch patties.
6. Grill the skewers for 6 to 12 minutes, flipping the skewers every 3 minutes. The skewers are done when their exterior forms a caramelized crust. Transfer the skewers onto a platter.
7. Place the patties on the grill or in a grill basket. Grill the patties for 6 to 12 minutes, flipping every 3 minutes. The patties are done when their exterior forms a caramelized crust.
8. To serve, divide the lettuce and herbs between two or three large serving platters. Distribute the noodles among plates and garnish with peanuts and fried shallots, if using. Divide the patties and pork belly slices among bowls, pour ¼ cup nước chấm over the meat, then add a few pieces of pickled carrots and daikon to each bowl. Serve a plate of noodles with a bowl of pork to each diner and place the lettuce and herbs in the middle of the table to share.

THE ULTIMATE THỊT HEO QUAY (CRISPY PORK BELLY)

This recipe is based on one that goes back to one of my sisters, Lan, who often made a huge slab for family gatherings. It was so good that the majority of it would be gone before dinner, snatched up by the kids as soon as she cut into it. The funny thing is, before we immigrated to the US, crispy pork belly wasn't something we made at home. In Việt Nam, we got our belly fix at our favorite spot for roast suckling pig, and it was only when we couldn't find a comparable restaurant here that my sister was compelled to figure out how to recreate it in her kitchen.

The best crispy pork belly is a celebration of flavors and textures, starting with a cap of puffed, crunchy skin followed by a layer of melting fat, then, finally, beautifully tender meat. There is a true art to preparing the belly so it crisps perfectly while staying juicy.

We offer a few techniques here: Because moisture is the enemy of crisp, we start by salting the belly and drying it out completely overnight in the fridge. When it's time to cook, we score the slab and reinforce it with a few strategically placed skewers; that helps the pork stay flat and the skin to roast and puff evenly, rather than contracting and curling. All that said, don't be daunted by the process. More than anything, the key is to pay attention. Every oven has its own intricacies and hot spots, and getting to know your oven's quirks will be the dif-

ference between a pork skin that crackles and one that merely snaps. Once roasted, it will be hard not to dive right in, just as the kids do, but it is even better when dipped into nước chấm and served with steamed rice, vegetables, and soup to round out the meal.

SERVES 6 TO 8

1 (3-pound) slab center-cut skin-on pork belly
4 teaspoons Red Boat Salt or kosher salt, divided
2 teaspoons five-spice powder

FOR SERVING

Steamed rice
All-Purpose Nước Chấm, Điệp Pham's Nước Chấm, or Nước Chấm Gừng (Ginger Dipping Sauce) (pages 275, 277, and 280)

The day before roasting: Salt the skin

1. Place the pork belly skin-side down on a cutting board, then trim the belly so it's the same thickness throughout. This is crucial: If one side is thicker than the other, the pork belly will roast unevenly, resulting in areas that will be burnt and others that will not puff properly during roasting.
2. Turn the pork belly skin-side up. Rub the pork belly skin with 3 teaspoons of the salt.
3. Place the pork belly, skin-side up, on a wire rack fitted into a baking sheet. Leave uncovered in the refrigerator overnight.

Marinate and roast the pork belly

4. Remove the pork belly from the refrigerator and use a paper towel to wipe off the salt and moisture from the skin. Be thorough: The drier the pork skin, the crispier it will be. (You can also return the pork belly to the refrigerator, uncovered, for another day to allow the skin to dry out even more.)
5. Use a skewer to poke holes all over skin. These perforations will help the skin puff up and become crisp, so the more perforations, the better.
6. Turn the pork over, skin-side down, then make 4 shallow cuts along the grain to score the belly into even strips roughly 1½ to 2 inches wide. Press one palm to keep the pork belly steady, then run a skewer through the

→ *continued*

belly between each score mark—a total of 5 skewers through the belly. With the belly now reinforced, go over your score lines again, this time slicing the meat about halfway down. Rotate the belly 180 degrees, and run a skewer every 2 inches across the slab. You should end up with one whole block of belly bound together with horizontal and vertical skewers. Trim any part of the skewers protruding from the sides of the slab.

7. In a small bowl, combine the five-spice powder with the remaining 1 teaspoon of salt. Coat the underside and side of the belly strips with the rub. Do not apply any rub to the belly's skin.

Check to make sure your five-spice powder hasn't gone stale. With so few ingredients in the salt rub, fresh five-spice will make a big difference in flavor.

8. Stack two sheets of aluminum foil on top of each other on your work surface. Place the belly skin-side up on top of the foil, then fold up the sides to create an open-face box that snugly encases the belly.
9. Let the pork belly rest at room temperature for 1 hour. While it rests, preheat the oven to 250°F. Line a baking sheet with aluminum foil (to make cleanup easier) and place a wire rack on top.
10. Place the aluminum-wrapped belly on the wire rack–lined baking sheet and put it in the oven on the highest rack. Position the pork toward the back of the oven. Roast for 2½ hours.
11. After 2½ hours, raise the oven temperature to 400°F and roast for 40 minutes, or until the skin has crisped and puffed.
12. When the skin has puffed, turn off the oven and prop open the oven door so it's slightly ajar. Leave the pork in the oven to roast for another 40 minutes in the residual heat.
13. After 40 minutes, take the pork belly out of the oven and remove the skewers. Slice and serve warm or at room temperature with the steamed rice and nước chấm.

THỊT BA RỌI CUỐN (PORK ROAST)

This pork roast is an adaptation of my mother's recipe for thịt ba rọi cuốn, where she would tightly roll a slab of pork belly and cook it in boiling water. Once cooled, she'd very thinly slice the pork and use the slices to make cold cut sandwiches. As we reconstructed her recipe, we decided to try roasting the pork instead—an option that was not available to her, as she didn't have an oven—and the result was absolutely outstanding. Served hot, it makes for a showstopping centerpiece at dinner; we suggest carving it right at the table and pairing the roast with the Caesar Salad (page 68) for a perfect meal with close friends or family. Note that you'll need a spool of kitchen twine to prevent the pork from unraveling as it cooks, and that you will very likely have leftovers. What to do with them? Make bánh mì for the next day's lunch, of course!

SERVES 4 TO 6

2 bay leaves
2 star anise pods
2 tablespoons vegetable oil
1 tablespoon annatto seeds (see page 25)
3 pounds center-cut pork belly, skin removed and trimmed to about 6 x 9 inches long

2 tablespoons minced garlic
2 tablespoons Red Boat Fish Sauce
2 tablespoons granulated sugar
1 teaspoon ground black pepper
1 teaspoon sesame oil

FOR SERVING (OPTIONAL)

All-Purpose Nước Chấm, Điệp Pham's Nước Chấm, or Nước Chấm Gừng (Ginger Dipping Sauce) (pages 275, 277, and 280)

→ *continued*

The day before roasting: Marinate the pork

1. Crush the bay leaves and break apart the star anise pods and add them to a small sauce pot. Add vegetable oil and, over medium heat, gently toast the spices for 5 minutes.
2. Add the annatto seeds to the pot, then turn off the heat and cover. Let the spices steep together for 20 minutes. Set aside to cool.
3. Place the pork belly in a large resealable bag and add the minced garlic, fish sauce, sugar, and black pepper. Strain the cooled spiced oil and add it to the bag, too. Seal and massage the marinade into the belly.
4. Place the bag on a baking sheet and transfer to the fridge. Marinate the belly for at least 24 hours, or up to 3 days. Flip the pork belly every 12 hours.

Truss the pork

5. Begin by cutting nine strings of cotton twine, each 18 inches in length.
6. Lay the strings in vertical, parallel lines across a 9 x 13-inch baking sheet, about ½ inch apart.
7. Remove the pork belly from the marinade and place, fat-side down, with the shorter side across all 9 strings.
8. Carefully roll the pork belly into a tight log and secure it with the strings underneath. Cut the excess twine and discard.

Roast the pork

9. Place the trussed pork on a wire rack placed in a 9 x 12-inch baking sheet (if you don't have a 9 x 12-inch pan, choose one that's the closest in size to the pork).
10. Put the pan on the middle rack of a cold oven. Set the oven at 250°F and roast until the temperature of the pork on an instant-read thermometer inserted into the thickest part registers at least 145°F, about 2 hours.
11. Remove the pork and increase the heat to 425°F. When the oven comes to temperature, return the pork to the oven and roast until the pork is well browned, 15 to 30 minutes.
12. Turn off the oven, but keep the roast there to finish cooking for another 30 minutes in the oven's residual heat.
13. Remove the baking sheet from the oven. Baste the roast with the sesame oil and transfer to a platter.

Make a sauce with the drippings and serve

14. Remove the wire rack from the baking sheet and add ½ cup water to the sheet. Carefully place it on the stovetop over medium heat and bring to a simmer.
15. Use a spatula to lift up all the drippings stuck to the pan. Continue simmering until the drippings dissolve into a sauce, about 5 minutes.
16. Pour the sauce into a measuring cup. If there's a lot of fat, carefully tilt the cup to remove as much (or as little!) fat as you'd like.
17. To serve, carve the roast into ½-inch medallions and remove the string. Finish with a generous pour of the sauce over the medallions and serve, if you wish, with nước chấm.

CƠM TẤM

(SEARED PORK CHOPS WITH BROKEN RICE)

Cơm tấm is one of Việt Nam's quintessential street foods. On the streets of almost every major city in the country, you can find cơm tấm vendors shrouded in plumes of smoke as they grill marinated chops on charcoal-fed braziers breathing blistering-hot fire. They are true masters of the grill, as the chops are so thin that it takes deft hands to control the heat. It also takes the sharpest of cooking instincts to know precisely when to pull the chops off the flame before they dry out. At home, you can ensure juicy chops every time by first brining the meat for a day or two and then giving them a quick sear in butter. If you want to use thick-cut chops instead, sear them on each side, then place them in a 350°F oven for 5 to 10 minutes, until the center reaches 145°F. For plating, we suggest serving the chops with broken rice and a warm slice of chả trứng hấp (steamed pork and wood ear meat loaf).

SERVES 4

4 bone-in pork chops (about ⅓ inch thick)
2 tablespoons minced garlic
2 tablespoons finely minced lemongrass (see Box, opposite)
1½ tablespoons granulated sugar
1 teaspoon ground black pepper
2 tablespoons Red Boat Fish Sauce
4 tablespoons butter, divided

FOR SERVING

4 to **6** cups cooked broken rice
All-Purpose Nước Chấm or Điệp Pham's Nước Chấm (pages 275 and 277)
Chả Trứng Hấp (Steamed Egg Meat Loaf, page 46) (optional)
Pickled Cabbage (page 264)

1. Place the pork chops, garlic, lemongrass, sugar, black pepper, and fish sauce in a large resealable bag. Squeeze as much air out as possible and seal the bag. Put the bag on a plate or tray and refrigerate for 24 to 48 hours.
2. Place a medium (ideally, 12-inch) heavy-bottomed pan over medium-high heat. Add 2 tablespoons of butter to the pan. Once the butter starts to bubble and brown, add two pork chops to the pan, making sure they're not too close to each other so they can sear properly (if they're too close, the chops will steam instead of sear). Sear the chops until browned, about 2 to 4 minutes, then flip and sear the other sides for another 2 to 4 minutes.
3. Transfer the chops to a platter. Add 2 tablespoons water to deglaze the pan, using a silicone spatula to scrape up any bits stuck to the pan. Pour the pan juices over the chops.
4. Wipe the pan clean with a towel and repeat with the remaining chops and remaining 2 tablespoons butter.
5. To serve, place each pork chop over broken rice on a large plate, along with a small of bowl of nước chấm, a slice of chả trứng hấp, and some pickled cabbage.

HOW TO MINCE LEMONGRASS

Lemongrass stalks can be rather tough and woody, which is why it's often strained out of a dish before serving. But if you mince the stalks as fine as possible, the lemongrass will meld into, say, a marinade, and won't need to be removed before serving. Here's how: Remove the dry outer layers of the lemongrass and wash off any residual dirt. Chop off and discard about ¼ inch of the lemongrass base. With a very sharp knife, thinly slice the lemongrass into coins—the thinner the better. Continue slicing until halfway up the lemongrass stalk, then discard the remaining top (the majority of the oils are in the bottom half of the stalk, so there's no need to use the tops). Chop the lemongrass coins into a fine mince. It's ready for use.

RIBS AND RICE

These ribs are a favorite of ours, a reminder of past summers when the kids would spend hours in the pool while we set up the grill. Few things got them out of the water faster than hearing the ribs were done, at which point they'd suddenly appear at the grill, sopping wet, goggles shoved up high on their foreheads, sneaking in a rib or two. Made with a marinade that requires just seven ingredients you probably have in your pantry—including, of course, fish sauce—these are ribs that stick to your teeth. They'll come off the grill burnished a beautiful bronze and flecked with char, ready to be served with a simple plate of rice (if the kids don't get to it first). Alternatively, if we're planning on a larger meal, we'll toss the ribs on the grill early on: They're a pretty fine snack to nibble on while waiting for everything else to get on the table.

SERVES 4 TO 6

6 scallions, chopped into 1-inch lengths
6 cloves garlic, chopped
1 tablespoon plus **1** teaspoon granulated sugar
1 teaspoon ground black pepper
3 tablespoons Red Boat Fish Sauce
1 teaspoon soy sauce
2 tablespoons grapeseed, canola, vegetable, or other neutral oil
3 pounds baby back ribs

FOR SERVING

Red Boat Scallion Oil (page 285)
Steamed rice
All-Purpose Nước Chấm or Điệp Pham's Nước Chấm (page 275 and 277)
Pickled Cabbage (page 264)

1. In the bowl of a small food processor or a bowl with an immersion blender, combine the scallions, garlic, sugar, pepper, fish sauce, soy sauce, and oil and grind into a fine paste. Set aside.
2. Trim and discard the silver skin and excess fat from the ribs, then cut the rack into individual ribs and place them in a large resealable storage bag.
3. Pour the marinade into the bag, then seal and massage the marinade into the ribs. Place the ribs in the refrigerator and marinate for at least 4 hours, or up to 2 days.
4. **If grilling:** Preheat the grill over medium. Grill the ribs for 15 minutes, then flip and grill for another 15 minutes. The ribs are done when the flesh starts to shrink away from the bone.

   If roasting: Preheat the oven to 375°F. Place the ribs on a wire rack set atop a baking sheet. Place the baking sheet on the top rack of the oven and roast for 40 minutes, rotating the pan halfway through the cooking time to ensure even cooking. The ribs are done when the flesh shrinks away from the bone.
5. Remove the ribs from the grill or oven. Top the ribs with a few spoonfuls of the scallion oil and serve with rice, nước chấm, and pickles.

WONTONS IN SOUP

Making wontons is a time-honored Phamily tradition that goes back to the kids' childhoods. The adults would make the filling, then the kids would sort themselves into different roles: One peeled the wrappers, the other two filled and shaped the dumplings. It sometimes took a few (dozen) wontons to get the shaping right, but once the wonton workflow was in place, we could make dozens in no time. The wontons are delicious on their own, but we especially love them in a warm bowl of chicken broth drizzled with sesame oil. This simple, no-fuss recipe makes quite a few wontons; it can be easily halved, but we suggest making them all and freezing any uncooked wontons. To do so, place the uncooked wontons on a parchment-lined baking sheet dusted with flour, then freeze. Once the wontons are individually frozen, they can be stored in resealable freezer bags for up to six months, ready to go the next time the wonton craving hits. The wontons can be cooked directly out of the freezer—just boil them for a few extra minutes to cook through.

MAKES 80 TO 90 WONTONS

WONTONS

1 pound ground pork
1 pound peeled and deveined shrimp, minced
1 teaspoon granulated sugar
2 teaspoons white pepper
2 tablespoons cornstarch
1 teaspoon sesame oil
2½ tablespoons Red Boat Fish Sauce
1 tablespoon plus **1** teaspoon sake
2 teaspoons minced ginger
1 cup finely chopped scallions, green and white parts
1 egg
2 (12-ounce) packets Hong Kong–style wonton wrappers, or enough wrappers to make 80 to 90 wontons

SOUP

1½ quarts Chicken or Pork Stock (pages 292 and 294), or store-bought
½ cup thinly sliced scallions
1 (1-pound) package egg noodles, cooked according to the manufacturer's instructions (optional)
1 cup chopped cilantro
Sesame oil

→ *continued*

Make the wontons

1. In a large mixing bowl, add the pork, shrimp, sugar, pepper, cornstarch, sesame oil, fish sauce, sake, ginger, scallions, and egg. Use your hands to thoroughly combine all the ingredients.
2. Prepare your wonton assembly line: A bowl of water, as many teaspoons or small spoons as there are people to help fill the dumplings, and a parchment-lined baking sheet.
3. Dip your finger in the bowl of water and lightly wet the edges of a wonton wrapper. Place about 1 teaspoon of the filling in the middle of it.
4. Fold the wrapper in half on the diagonal to form a triangle shape. Working from the filling outward, gently press both sides of the wrapper together, gently pushing out any air pockets as you do so. Press firmly around the edges to seal the wonton.
5. Lay the filled wonton on the parchment-lined baking sheet, making sure the wontons aren't touching each other (if they do, they may stick).
6. Repeat until all the filling is used. Freeze any wontons you won't be cooking immediately.

Assemble the soup

7. In a medium pot over medium-high heat, bring 4 quarts of water to a boil. (Because the starch in the wonton wrappers will cloud the cooking liquid, we boil the wontons in water rather than in the stock, so the stock stays clear.)
8. As the water comes to a boil, in another pot, pour in the chicken stock and place it over medium heat. Bring the stock to a boil as well, then bring the heat down to very low so the stock is at a bare simmer.
9. Once the water begins to boil, slide six wontons into the water. Boil until the wontons float, about 4 minutes. Use a strainer to lift the wontons carefully from the water. Gently shake the strainer a few times to drain any excess water from the dumplings.
10. Transfer the wontons to a serving bowl. Add a handful of thinly sliced scallions, and the noodles if using. Pour 1½ cups stock into each serving and garnish with chopped cilantro and a few drops of sesame oil. Serve immediately.

MALAI KITCHEN'S FIVE-SPICE PORK BELLY

Braden and Yasmin Wages, the owners of Malai Kitchen with three locations in and around Dallas, are wonderful hosts, and I always enjoy my visits to their restaurants. We're fortunate to count them among our fans—in fact, a few years back, they visited our barrel house during one of their trips to Việt Nam, bringing along a few members of their team to join in on the tour. At Malai Kitchen, they put their spin on a range of Thai and Vietnamese dishes, and this recipe is a great showcase of the sort of cooking they do there. The star of the dish is pork belly, braised slowly over several hours in a sauce outfitted with fish sauce, oyster sauce, and a healthy shake of five spice, then served over vermicelli with tofu and mushrooms. The result: a rich, deeply comforting bowl of noodles.

SERVES 6

½ pound soft or semi-soft tofu, diced into 1-inch cubes
¼ cup cornstarch
Vegetable oil
2 pounds pork belly
¼ cup Red Boat Fish Sauce, plus additional to taste
¼ cup honey
¼ cup oyster sauce
1 tablespoon five-spice powder
4 cups Pork Stock (page 294) or water, plus more as necessary
12 shiitake mushrooms, washed and stemmed

For serving
Cooked rice vermicelli noodles
6 soft-boiled eggs
Chopped chives
Black pepper

→ *continued*

1. Coat the diced tofu in the cornstarch. Place a medium sauté pan over high heat and add ½-inch of oil. When the oil begins to smoke, carefully add the tofu and pan-fry until slightly crispy on all sides, about 5 minutes. Remove the tofu from the pan and set aside.
2. Trim the pork belly of any excess fat. In a large sauté pan set over high heat, pour a tablespoon of oil. When the oil begins to smoke, add the pork belly and sear until golden brown on each side, about 4 minutes total.
3. In a large Dutch oven or braising pan, make the braising broth by combining the fish sauce, honey, oyster sauce, five-spice, and stock. Bring to a simmer over medium heat.
4. Once the broth begins to simmer, place the pork belly in the pot, making sure it's completely submerged in the liquid, adding additional stock if necessary. Cover the pot tightly with a lid and simmer for 4 hours, checking periodically to ensure there is enough broth.
5. After the first 3 hours, add the tofu and mushrooms and cover again.
6. After the fourth hour, the pork belly should be very tender and pull apart easily, the broth should be reduced by half, and the pork should have rendered its fat. Skim the fat from the top of broth and taste the broth. Add an extra dash of fish sauce, if needed, to perfect the seasoning.
7. Portion the noodles and broth among six bowls and top each with pork belly, tofu, mushrooms, and an egg. Garnish with chopped chives and cracked black pepper and serve.

BRYANT NG'S CHARCUTERIE FRIED RICE

Bryant Ng is the chef behind Cassia in Santa Monica, a lively Southeast Asian brasserie that he co-owns with Kim Luu-Ng. Bryant and Kim are one of our longtime fans—in fact, we were all in an episode of the PBS show *Migrant Kitchen* together! I've always appreciated Bryant for his support, especially very early on, when he offered valuable feedback on our fish sauce. He was a huge advocate of our Red Boat Salt, so much so that we collaborated with him recently to create a special Cassia Salt Rub. During a trip to Việt Nam in 2013, Bryant visited the barrel house, and we bonded over our obsession for the crab fried rice at a stand at the night market. As it happens, one option among the stellar dishes Bryant makes at Cassia is also fried rice, like this one here, studded with singed pieces of house-cured lạp xưởng and Chinese bacon with a bit of salted cod for another layer of savoriness. For best results, use rice left over from last night's dinner, as the grains will have lost some moisture and be drier than freshly steamed rice—all the better for frying. And because each component of the fried rice cooks so quickly, be sure to have all the ingredients prepared and ready to go before you flick on the flame. To fry, Bryant recommends using a wok, as it can handle very, very high heat.

→ *continued*

SERVES 2

1 tablespoon lard
1 tablespoon minced or pureed garlic
1 tablespoon shallots, minced or pureed
1 Thai chile, sliced into rounds
¼ cup lạp xưởng, sliced large enough to make a presence
¼ cup Chinese bacon or lardons
2 tablespoons salt cod, soaked in water to reconstitute, then diced
2 cups cooked jasmine rice, preferably one day old
½ tablespoon Red Boat Fish Sauce
¼ cup shredded iceberg lettuce

GARNISH

2 tablespoons sliced scallion, green parts only
1 bunch cilantro

1. In a wok or a large sauté pan over high heat, heat the lard.
2. Add the garlic and shallot and stir. Cook them very briefly, just 10 seconds.
3. Add the Thai chile, lạp xưởng, bacon, and salt cod. Stir. Cook briefly, about 30 seconds.
4. Add the day-old rice and mix, tossing to combine the ingredients.
5. Season with fish sauce and cook until you have your desired texture of rice.
6. Add the lettuce at the end, then stir and toss to combine.
7. Plate the fried rice and garnish with scallion and sprigs of cilantro.

THE IMPORTANCE OF SALT

It's hard to overstate the importance of salt in making fish sauce. Salt is what we use to preserve the anchovies and their precious flavor after they're caught and hauled on deck. Once the anchovies are transferred into barrels, the salt continues to preserve the fish and aids the fermentation process as the fish break down into fish sauce.

We source our salt from the fields of Long Sơn, which is about 280 miles from Phú Quốc. It's an area especially rich in minerals, and, for many families in the area, salt harvesting goes back generations. The harvest begins when sea water is brought in and held in large, flat evaporation ponds. After about two weeks, the water will have evaporated, and the salt is ready to be collected. The process is completely manual: Using long wooden plows, harvesters in tall rubber boots push the salt, one long sweep at a time, into large pyramid-shaped piles. They start very, very early in the morning to avoid the worst of the day's heat and humidity, but even at that early hour, the sun is unforgiving. The entire process is incredibly meticulous and time-consuming, and each season's harvest is a testament to experienced, skilled hands. Once piled, the salt is left to dry out over a period of weeks or months, depending on its intended use, then stored in silos.

For fish sauce makers, salt preferences vary widely: Every producer has their own preferred grade, coarseness, moisture level, and source for salt. Every fish sauce maker also has their own personal methodology for salting the fish, including exactly how much salt to use. My early days of Red Boat were full of trials and errors as I worked with the Red Boat fishing crew and tinkered with various salts to find the right salt and the right ratio of salt to fish. This period of experimentation took an enormous amount of patience: Because the anchovies require several months to ferment, I wasn't able to taste the results of my experiments until nearly a year later. I did learn quickly, though, that the grade of salt mattered significantly. Lower grades of salt, left to dry for just a few weeks, are speckled with sand and grit. That salt is suitable for making fish sauce, but the impurities impart an unwelcome tannic flavor that remains in the sauce even when they're eventually filtered out. On the other hand, the highest grade of salt is left undisturbed for several months, during which time gravity does its work in drawing down (and out) the sand and grit. The salt's moisture level also reduces as more water evaporates, and it's not as harsh in flavor as the lower grade salt.

Unsurprisingly, the highest grade of salt is markedly more expensive than the lower grades. But for us, the quality and flavor of that high grade is worth that extra cost. The salt we order now is aged for about three months, and we order enough every year to reserve our lot and to make sure we're well stocked. (Salt is what I consider a single point of failure: We could have a fleet's worth of anchovies, but if we don't have enough salt to preserve them, then our entire process skids to a halt.)

Sometimes you can see the salt yourself, dancing at the very bottom of our fish sauce bottle after some of the liquid has evaporated. This precipitation is a completely natural process!

Using this high-grade salt has yielded an entirely unexpected benefit. After the fish sauce is drained and the anchovies removed from the fermentation barrels, the salt left behind is, as it turns out, thoroughly infused with the umami from the anchovies. In other words, it's absolutely delicious! So, rather than tossing it, we collect and dehydrate the salt into crystals and package it into jars. It makes for a great seasoning, and our fans mix it with other spices to create their own dry rubs. We're incredibly happy to be able to make the most of the salt. The labor it took to harvest it is not something we ever want to take for granted.

CHAPTER 7

CHICKEN & BEEF

ANN'S CHICKEN SOUP

This hearty chicken soup feels like a big bear hug. This is one of Ann's staples, and one she makes especially when any of us are feeling under the weather. The soup is full of hearty vegetables—Ann uses carrots, chayote (a gourd as crisp as an apple, with a low moisture content that makes it ideal for cooking in soups like this one), leeks, and celery, all of which we usually have in the fridge—but feel free to swap those out for what you have on hand in your crisper drawer. The addition of fish sauce right at the end gives the soup a comforting zip of savory flavor. For maximum restorative effect, use homemade chicken stock if you can, as it does make a huge difference in flavor. And while this soup is great with just the vegetables and chicken, we often add in a short variety of pasta, too, like orzo or farfalle.

SERVES 6

1 leek, white part only
¼ head green cabbage
1 medium chayote
1 to **2** celery stalks
1 pound boneless, skinless chicken thighs or breasts
½ large sweet onion, diced into ½-inch pieces
1 large carrot, peeled and sliced into ½-inch coins
2 cups Chicken Stock (page 292), or store-bought
1 teaspoon Red Boat Salt or 1 to 2 tablespoons Red Boat Fish Sauce

→ *continued*

Prepare the chicken and vegetables

1. Cut the leek lengthwise, then cut and remove the top and green portions. Rinse the remaining white portion to remove any visible dirt. Cut the white part of the leek into ½-inch pieces. Fill a large bowl with water, add the leek pieces, and let them sit for 10 minutes to remove any remaining dirt and grit between the layers. Drain and set aside.
2. Core and coarsely chop the cabbage leaves. Set both cabbage leaves and core aside.
3. Slice about ½ inch off the very top of the chayote. Rub the cut end of that piece against the cut end of the chayote. As you do so, the vegetable's white, bitter, sticky sap will come to the surface; rinse off the sap and repeat for about 5 minutes, or until the sap no longer appears. Rinse one final time, then peel the chayote and cut it in half lengthwise. Using a spoon, scoop out the chayote core, then dice each half into ½-inch cubes and set aside.
4. Using a peeler, remove the fibrous strings from the celery. Slice the celery into ½-inch pieces (you should end up with 1 cup of sliced celery). Set aside.
5. Cube the chicken into 1-inch pieces. Set aside.

Make the broth

6. Pour 2 quarts of water into a 5-quart pot. Bring the water to a boil, then add the cabbage core. Let boil for 5 minutes, then remove and discard the core.
7. Add the leeks, celery, and onion, then bring the water back to a boil. Reduce the heat and simmer for 20 minutes. Skim off any impurities that float up.
8. Add the chayote, chicken, and carrots. Bring the pot back up to a boil, then reduce the heat to a bare simmer. Simmer for 20 minutes, skimming off any impurities that float up.
9. Cut a piece of chicken to make sure it's cooked through. If the chicken is not yet cooked through, simmer for another 5 to 10 minutes.
10. Add the chicken stock and bring the pot back to a boil, then reduce to a simmer. Taste a piece of carrot to test its texture: At this point, the carrots should be cooked but still firm. If you prefer your carrots and chayote more tender, cook for another 10 to 20 minutes.
11. Add the cabbage leaves and 1 teaspoon Red Boat Salt (or 1 tablespoon fish sauce) and cook for another 5 minutes. Taste and add more fish sauce if you'd like. Remove the pot from heat and serve.

RAGU GÀ (CHICKEN RAGU)

Some people like tomato soup with grilled cheese—we like tomato and chicken stew with a baguette. This ragu is not often served in restaurants, as it's an especially homey dish, and one that always reminds the kids of their childhoods. In preparing the chicken, we chop the meat across the bone with a heavy cleaver and a firm, confident hand. If you prefer not to do the chopping yourself, you often can find freshly chopped chicken packaged in the meat section of Asian markets. Alternatively, you can use boneless chicken thighs instead.

SERVES 4 TO 6

- **3** pounds skin-on chicken legs
- **2** to **3** tablespoons Red Boat Fish Sauce, divided
- **1** teaspoon ground black pepper
- **2** tablespoons olive oil
- **2** tablespoons butter
- **2** cups diced yellow onions
- **3** tablespoons tomato paste
- **½** pound russet potatoes, peeled and diced into 1-inch cubes
- **2** bay leaves
- **2** to **3** cups Chicken Stock (page 292)
- **½** pound cremini mushrooms, cleaned and quartered

FOR SERVING

Bánh mì, baguette, or other crusty bread

→ *continued*

1. Remove any excess skin hanging off the side of the chicken legs. Using a cleaver or other heavy knife and a firm hand, chop the chicken legs across the bones into large pieces. Season the pieces with 1 tablespoon of fish sauce and black pepper. Marinate for 10 minutes.
2. Combine the olive oil and butter in a large pot over medium-high heat. When the butter starts to foam, add half the chicken and sear on each side for 2 minutes. Transfer the chicken to a mixing bowl. Sear the rest of the chicken and transfer it to the mixing bowl.
3. Once all the chicken is seared, add the onions to the pot and sauté until browned, about 10 minutes. Use a spatula to lift any bits stuck to the bottom of the pot.
4. Add the tomato paste and cook for 5 minutes, stirring frequently to prevent the paste from scorching.
5. Return the chicken to the pot and mix thoroughly to coat the chicken evenly in the tomato-onion mixture. Reduce the heat to low, cover, and cook for 10 minutes.
6. After 10 minutes, remove the cover and add the potatoes and bay leaves to the pot. Add enough chicken stock to cover about 80 percent of the chicken and potatoes. Bring the pot to a boil, then reduce the heat to a simmer. Cover and simmer until the potatoes can be easily pierced with a fork, 5 to 10 minutes.
7. Add the mushrooms and simmer, uncovered, until they're cooked through and tender, 2 to 5 minutes. Taste the broth and add up to 2 more tablespoons of fish sauce if you feel the broth isn't salty enough. Remove the bay leaves and serve the ragu with plenty of bread.

CHICKEN TINGA

We use nước mắm (fish sauce) very often in the Vietnamese braises we make at home. Cloaked in the braising liquid, it brings a subtle but irreplaceably pronounced umami to the fore. And, as it turns out, what works for Vietnamese braises also works for many other non-Vietnamese braises, too! Here we add our fish sauce to chicken tinga, a dish that hails from Puebla, Mexico. The fish sauce plays a supporting, but crucial, role to the umami-rich tomatoes that are the foundation of the braise. The entire dish comes together in less than an hour, including the time it takes to poach the chicken. Serve the tinga with a big stack of corn tortillas and lots of salsa to make it a proper taco night.

SERVES 4 TO 6

2 pounds boneless chicken thighs
3 bay leaves, divided
1 teaspoon kosher salt
2 dried guajillo chiles, stems and seeds removed
3 tablespoons canola, rice bran, grapeseed, or other neutral oil
½ pound yellow onion, diced
1 tablespoon minced garlic
1 teaspoon ground cumin
¾ pound cherry tomatoes
1 tablespoon chopped fresh oregano
2 tablespoons Red Boat Fish Sauce, plus additional to taste

FOR SERVING

1 cup thinly sliced red onions
½ cup crema fresca or sour cream
2 limes, cut into wedges
1 avocado, peeled, pitted and thinly sliced
1 cup chopped cilantro
2 cups thinly sliced cabbage
1 stack corn tortillas

→ *continued*

1. In a pot, combine the chicken thighs, 1 bay leaf, salt, and just enough water to cover the chicken. Bring the pot to a boil, then reduce the heat and poach the thighs on low until the chicken is cooked through, 15 to 20 minutes. Once the chicken is cooked, remove the pot from the heat and let the chicken cool in the cooking liquid.
2. As the chicken cools, cut the chiles into 2-inch pieces. Add the chiles and 3 cups of water to a small pot. Bring to a boil, then remove the pot from the heat and cover. Steep the chiles for at least 10 minutes.
3. While the chiles steep, in another pot, heat the oil over medium heat. Add the yellow onion, garlic, and cumin. Sauté until the onions break down, about 15 minutes, stirring occasionally to prevent the onions from scorching.
4. After the chiles have steeped for at least 10 minutes, drain, rinse, and put them in a blender. Transfer the sautéed onions to the blender and add the tomatoes and oregano. Puree the mixture to a smooth sauce.
5. Pour the sauce back into the pot that was used to sauté the onions. Add ¾ cup of the chicken's poaching liquid, the remaining 2 bay leaves, and the fish sauce. Bring the pot to a boil, then reduce the heat and simmer for 15 minutes.
6. Meanwhile, remove the chicken from the poaching liquid and shred. After the sauce has simmered for 15 minutes, add the shredded chicken. Simmer for another 10 minutes to allow the chicken to soak in the sauce.
7. As the chicken simmers in the sauce, mellow out the bite of the raw red onions by soaking the slices in a small bowl with just enough water to cover.
8. After 10 minutes, taste the chicken and add a splash or two of fish sauce if you think it needs it. If the tinga is thinner than you'd like at this point, continue simmering for a few more minutes until it reaches your preferred consistency. Remove the bay leaves.
9. Serve the tinga family style in the pot or transfer it to a serving dish. Drain the sliced red onions and serve them with the tinga, alongside the crema fresca, lime wedges, avocado, cilantro, cabbage, and tortillas.

RED BOAT GINGER-CILANTRO FRIED CHICKEN

The key to our succulent and savory fried chicken is all in the brine. The foundation is tangy buttermilk; to that, we add a few very special ingredients: ginger, cilantro, and (of course) our fish sauce. Cilantro is common in many Asian fried chicken renditions, and we like using the cilantro roots because they have a robust, heartier flavor than the leaves by themselves. If cilantro roots aren't available at your local grocer or farmers market, you can use cilantro leaves and stems instead. Thai basil also will work very well. To make the most of the brine, we strongly suggest brining the pieces for at least 8 hours, or overnight. That does require a bit of planning, but preparing in advance will be worth it. The longer the chicken takes in the brine, the more tender and flavorful it will be once fried. Use a small bird, as the pieces will cook through in a shorter amount of time than larger ones. That, in turn, will result in a juicier fried chicken. The chicken is terrific on its own, but reaches new heights of flavor when dunked in our Peanut-Coconut Nước Chấm. Be sure to make plenty of that dipping sauce for the table.

SERVES 4

1 (2½-pound) whole chicken or 2½ pounds chicken pieces

BUTTERMILK BRINE

1 cup buttermilk
1 cup cilantro roots
1 shallot
1 egg
2 tablespoons Red Boat Fish Sauce
4 cloves garlic
1 (1-inch) piece of ginger
1 to **3** Thai chiles, seeds and ribs removed if desired, roughly chopped (optional)
1 teaspoon apple cider vinegar

→ *continued*

FOR FRYING

2 cups all-purpose flour
1 cup sweet rice flour
1 tablespoon Red Boat Salt or kosher salt
1 tablespoon ground black pepper
1 teaspoon baking powder
Lard or oil with a high smoke point, like canola, peanut, rice bran, or grapeseed

FOR SERVING

Peanut-Coconut Nước Chấm (page 281)

Day 1: Brine the chicken

1. If using a whole chicken, butcher the chicken into 10 parts: 2 wings, 2 drumsticks, 2 thighs, and 4 breasts (cut the 2 breasts in half).
2. In a blender, add all the buttermilk brine ingredients. Blend until the mixture is smooth.
3. Place the chicken pieces in a large resealable storage bag. Carefully pour in the buttermilk brine. Remove the excess air from the bag and seal. Massage the brine into the chicken.
4. Place the bag on a large plate or baking sheet and let the chicken brine overnight in the refrigerator.

Day 2: Fry the chicken

5. In a large mixing bowl, combine the all-purpose flour, rice flour, salt, black pepper, and baking powder. Whisk well to insure all the dry ingredients are thoroughly mixed.
6. Quickly remove chicken pieces from the brine and roll them in the seasoned flour. Don't worry about draining the chicken before putting it into flour: The flour will clump in areas where there is excess brine, but the uneven surface, will result in a delicious, jagged crust. Use both hands to press the flour into the chicken. Place the chicken on a baking sheet and let the coating set for 20 minutes. Alternatively, transfer the baking sheet to the refrigerator and let the coating set for up to 24 hours.
7. Set a wire rack into a baking sheet. Fill a deep cast-iron skillet with 3 inches of frying oil. Bring the oil to 350°F on a deep-fry thermometer.
8. Working in batches, slowly—and carefully—slide the chicken pieces into the oil. The oil temperature will drop to around 300°F, which is fine; between 300° and 325°F is the ideal temperature range for frying chicken. Don't crowd the skillet; if you do so, the oil temperature will drop too much and the chicken won't fry properly.
9. Fry the chicken for 4 minutes, then flip and fry for another 4 minutes. Flip the chicken two more times, frying for two minutes each time, until golden. The chicken is done when its internal temperature is 165°F when checked with an instant-read thermometer inserted into the thickest part of the chicken piece.
10. Transfer the chicken to the wire rack. Fry the remaining chicken. Let the pieces drain on the rack for 5 minutes before serving with the peanut-coconut nước chấm.

CÀ RI GÀ (CHICKEN CURRY)

Packets of curry powder rattle in the kitchen drawers of many Vietnamese families, including ours. In fact, curry has been part of the Vietnamese kitchen for decades. As food historian Erica J. Peters writes in *Appetites and Aspirations in Vietnam*, curry was brought to Việt Nam from India during the French colonial period and was primarily served to the French stationed in Việt Nam, as they refused to eat rice—unless it was served with curry. Over the years, Vietnamese cooks re-adapted the dish, incorporating local ingredients like fish sauce and lemongrass. Our version of this homey chicken curry is fragrant with that lemongrass and dotted with islands of Japanese sweet potato. The curry powder and curry paste bring a bit of heat and plenty of spice; if you have a favorite curry powder and paste from your local Indian market, you can use them here. Otherwise, you can find both at large Asian markets like 99 Ranch Market and H Mart: D&D Gold and KTT are popular brands. We love having the curry with bánh mì, but you can also ladle it over noodles . . . or a bowl of rice.

SERVES 6

⅔ cup minced shallots
1 tablespoon minced garlic
1 tablespoon Red Boat Salt or kosher salt
2 teaspoons granulated sugar
2 teaspoons Madras curry powder
1 tablespoon Madras curry paste
3 pounds bone-in chicken breasts, thighs, or a combination of both
1½ pounds fresh tomatoes, or **8** ounces canned crushed tomatoes
3 tablespoons grapeseed, canola, vegetable, or other neutral oil, divided

1½ pounds Japanese sweet potato, peeled and cut into 1-inch cubes

¼ cup minced lemongrass (see page 20 on how to mince lemongrass)

3 bay leaves

3 to **4** Thai chiles, seeds and ribs removed if desired

16 ounces coconut water

1 cup coconut milk

½ pound yellow onion, sliced into ¼- to ½-inch wedges

3 tablespoons Red Boat Fish Sauce

FOR SERVING

1 to **2** baguettes, steamed rice, or **¾** pound bún tươi (fresh rice noodles), prepared according to package instructions

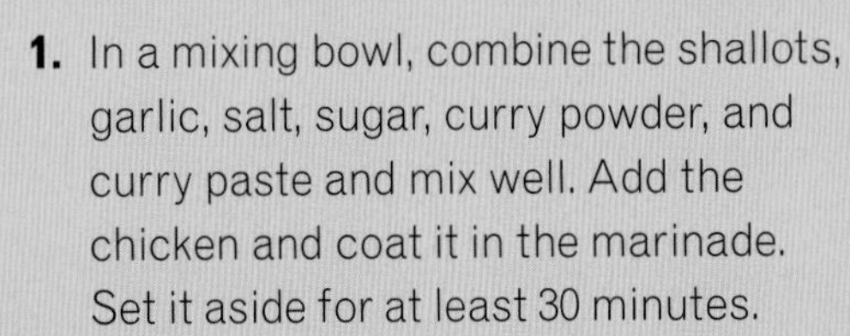

1. In a mixing bowl, combine the shallots, garlic, salt, sugar, curry powder, and curry paste and mix well. Add the chicken and coat it in the marinade. Set it aside for at least 30 minutes.
2. Slice a shallow cross on the bottoms of the tomatoes and place them in a pot with enough boiling water to cover. Boil the tomatoes just until their skins shrivel slightly, about 1 minute. Remove the tomatoes and, when they've cooled enough to handle, remove their skins. In a bowl, crush the peeled tomatoes and set aside. (If using canned tomatoes, skip this step.)
3. In a large pan, add 1 tablespoon of oil. When the oil begins to smoke, add the potatoes and fry until they're a light brown. (This will help prevent the potatoes from falling apart in the stew.) Set aside.
4. In a large pot or wok set over medium heat, add the remaining 2 tablespoons of oil. When the oil begins to smoke, add the lemongrass and sauté for 1 minute. Add the chicken and sauté the pieces until they're browned, then add the crushed tomatoes and bay leaves. Cover, lower the heat, and simmer for 10 minutes.
5. Remove the lid and add the potatoes and 3 of the chiles. Continue simmering, uncovered, for another 15 minutes.
6. Add the coconut water, coconut milk, onion, and fish sauce and bring to a boil over medium-low heat. Reduce the heat to low and simmer for another 10 to 15 minutes, until the chicken is tender and cooked through. Taste and, if you'd like a little more heat, add the remaining chile.
7. Remove the bay leaves and serve with the baguette, rice, or noodles.

MOM'S GÀ QUAY (ROAST CHICKEN)

This recipe is an adaptation of my mother's recipe for gà quay, which loosely translates as "rotisserie" or "roasted chicken." As with many home cooks in Việt Nam at the time, she didn't have access to an oven, so she steamed the chicken instead, then doused it in sizzling hot oil to brown and crisp the skin. The result was similar to what she would have made had it been cooked in the oven. Given that ovens are very much a part of American kitchens, we modified her technique slightly. We use the same flavorings she used—fish sauce, soy sauce, bay leaves—to marinate the bird, but we forego her oil method in favor of butterflying and roasting the chicken instead.

A note about equipment: We specify using an 8 x 10-inch wire rack fitted in a 9 x 13-inch baking sheet. If you use a larger baking sheet, the delicious juices that render during the roast will burn.

→ continued

SERVES 4

BASTING LIQUID

2 tablespoons diced garlic
½ cup diced shallots
¼ cup apple cider vinegar
¼ cup Red Boat Fish Sauce
¼ cup soy sauce
¼ teaspoon ground black pepper
2 bay leaves
2 tablespoons granulated sugar
¼ pound butter, cubed

SEASONING PASTE

1 cup roughly chopped white or yellow onions
5 cloves garlic, roughly chopped
2 teaspoons Red Boat Fish Sauce
2 tablespoons grapeseed, canola, vegetable, or other neutral oil
1 teaspoon ground black pepper

1 (2- to 3-pound) whole chicken

FOR SERVING

Nước Chấm Gừng (page 280)

Make the basting liquid

1. In a small saucepan, combine the garlic, shallots, vinegar, and ¼ cup of water. Bring the mixture to a boil and cook until the vinegar and water are almost all evaporated, about 5 minutes.
2. Add the fish sauce, soy sauce, black pepper, and bay leaves to the pan. Turn down the heat to low and keep the mixture at a low simmer for 15 minutes.
3. Transfer the mixture to a mixing bowl. Add the sugar and a few cubes of butter to the bowl, and stir gently to melt the butter. Repeat with the remaining butter.
4. Strain and discard the solids to make a velvety sauce. Cover and store in the refrigerator until needed.

Butterfly and marinate the chicken

5. In a blender, combine all the ingredients for the seasoning paste and process them. Set aside.
6. Remove the excess fat from around the thighs and neck of the chicken. Position the chicken breast-side up and with the legs facing away from you. Using sharp kitchen shears, start at the wishbone and cut along either side of the backbone to butterfly the chicken. Once done, the bird will lay flat.
7. Apply the seasoning paste underneath the skin of the chicken by tucking your hand between the skin and flesh, then rub the remaining paste all over the skin and interior of the chicken.
8. Place the chicken skin-side up in a dish lined with a wire rack and place

it, uncovered, in the refrigerator. Let the chicken marinate for at least 8 hours, or up to 2 days.

Roast the chicken

9. When you're ready to roast, preheat the oven to 375°F. Remove the chicken and the basting liquid from the refrigerator. Using a basting brush, apply a generous coat of the basting liquid onto the skin of the chicken until the skin is bronzed all over.
10. Place the chicken, skin-side up, on an 8 x 10-inch wire rack set in a 9 x 13-inch baking sheet, then place that on the lowest rack of the oven. Roast for 50 minutes.
11. After 50 minutes, remove the chicken from the oven. Position the rack to the highest position that can still accommodate the bird and increase the temperature to 425°F. While the oven gets to temperature, apply another coat of the basting liquid. Take care to coat as much surface as you can, including the sides of the chicken.
12. Once the oven has reached 425°F, return the chicken to the oven. Roast for an additional 15 minutes; every 5 minutes, apply another coat of the basting liquid. The total roasting time should be 65 minutes.

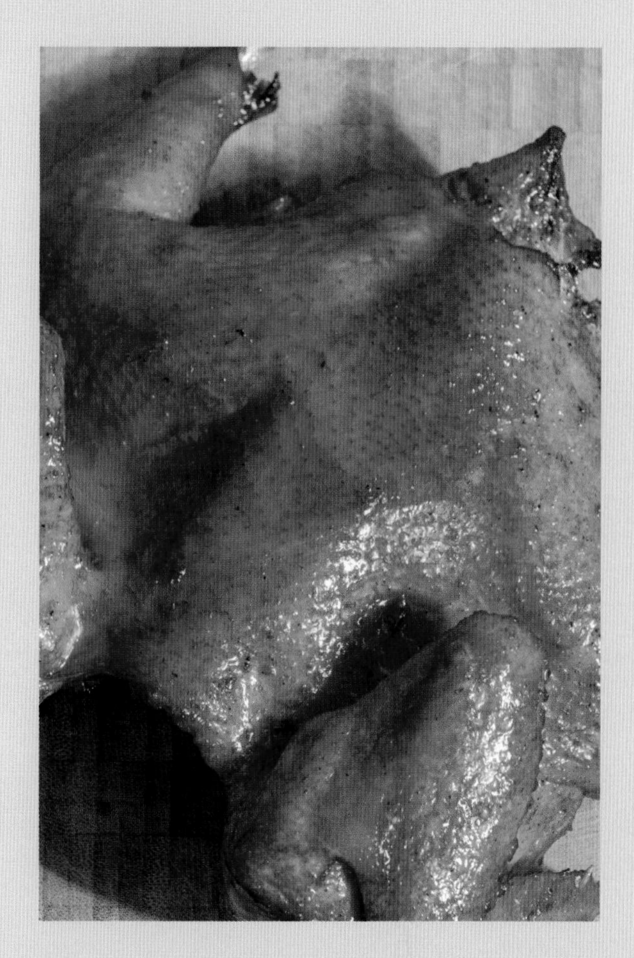

13. Remove the chicken from the oven and let it rest on the wire rack for 15 minutes before transferring it to a platter. Carefully pour the drippings that have collected in the baking sheet into a small ramekin or bowl.
14. Carve the chicken and serve with the drippings.

THE BARREL HOUSE

You can haul in the anchovies from the waters of Phú Quốc, you can salt them with the right amount and type of salt, but try, as many have, to ferment them anywhere other than in or right around Phú Quốc, and the resulting fish sauce won't be nearly as good as if the anchovies were fermented on the island itself. The difference in climate is that significant: There is no substitute for Phú Quốc's long, humid days, and it's this climate that plays a substantial role in making our fish sauce so special.

The centuries-old method of making fish sauce is to ferment the fish in tall wooden barrels constructed using wood from selected trees indigenous to the area, including one, the bời lời tree, that can tower to a height of some 65 feet (other trees that have been used to make the barrels are called dên dên, trai, and gỗ sao). These trees are especially suitable for making fish sauce for a few reasons. For one, they retain heat very well, making them excellent vessels for fermentation. And significantly, they're extraordinarily resilient. While other materials may degrade, buckle, and eventually leak from prolonged exposure to salt and liquid, the woods from these trees are not adversely affected. Properly maintained, barrels made with these woods will last decades.

Unfortunately, these barrels are the last of their kind. These trees now are protected by law and can no longer be cut down. Newer barrels are now made using woods from other local trees, though some producers have decided to forego the wooden barrels altogether and ferment the fish in cement tanks instead. It's worth noting that there are very few craftsmen remaining who still specialize in constructing the traditional wood barrels. I hope continued interest in fish sauce making will help keep this art alive.

When I was given the keys to the fish sauce factory that became Red Boat, it was a relatively small operation with just sixteen barrels. As Red Boat has grown, we've acquired more barrels; we now have a total of 190, stored across two tin-roofed facilities we call our barrel house. Each barrel is about ten feet tall, reinforced with thick belts of rattan, and capable of holding up to fourteen tons of salted anchovies.

Once the fish are loaded into the barrels, we rely entirely on the naturally occurring enzymes in the anchovies to break them down into sauce, not a culture or any other starter. As the

anchovies ferment, we depend on collected data as well as our own senses to routinely monitor how each barrel of fish sauce is coming along. This is crucial, as we don't use any sugars, flavor enhancers, food coloring, or any other additives to change the flavor or color of the sauce. Instead, the flavor of our fish sauce comes entirely from the fermented anchovies and salt. Achieving this pure flavor is a true combination of art and science, and consistency is key. When necessary, we blend the liquid from different barrels to ensure the flavor is consistent across batches.

We may also adjust the salt levels depending on how the sauce smells or tastes, and we routinely sample and taste how the sauce is progressing. Generally, after three months, the liquid is thin, bright red-orange, and a little rough around the edges on the palate. At six months, the sauce is more red than orange, and the salinity starts to mellow out. Sometime around 12 to 14 months, the color of liquid has deepened into an amber glaze, and the flavors of the anchovies and the sea reach their full spectrum of richness, balance, and nuance.

Overseeing this entire process is our manager, Hong, who has been with us since 2013. Led by Hong's experienced eye and palate, our team is constantly testing and tasting to ensure every batch of Red Boat is consistent and balanced.

When the fish sauce is finally ready, we drain it from the barrels and filter it. This first extraction of our fish sauce—nước mắm nhỉ—is the most flavorful and pure.

From there, the fish sauce is bottled, hits the shelves, and makes its way to your kitchen. Meanwhile, at the barrel house it's time to do it all over again with the next haul of anchovies.

40°N AND UMAMI

How much flavor is in our fish sauce? Quite a bit. The irreplaceable flavor of umami is produced by naturally occurring proteins in the anchovies; the more of these proteins, the higher the umami. To determine how much protein is in a liter of fish sauce, the industry measures the level of nitrogen in the liquid. The higher the nitrogen level, the higher the protein content, and the higher the umami. Thirty degrees of nitrogen per liter is considered quality fish sauce. We're proud to say that our fish sauce measures forty degrees of nitrogen per liter—hence the "40°N" you see on our bottles. For those familiar with fish sauce, forty degrees is also an Easter egg: evidence that indicates this fish sauce truly does come from Phú Quốc, as the island is the only place capable of naturally producing fish sauce with this level of nitrogen. That number is our commitment to quality and flavor.

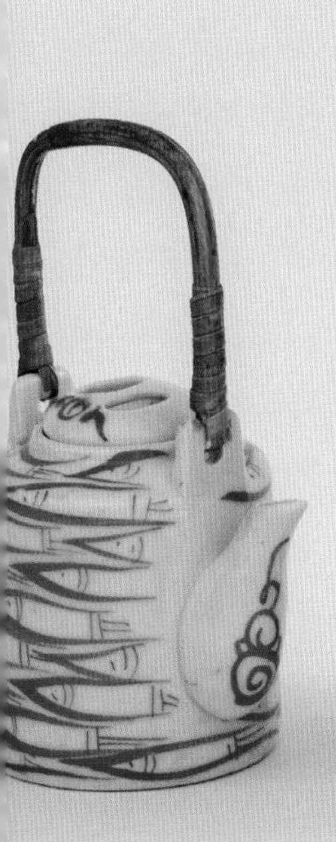

BURGERS WITH RED BOAT DRESSING

Here's a fun recipe for your next cookout. Our take on the classic American burger starts with the dressing, where fish sauce is stirred into mayonnaise and ketchup to create our own very special version of Thousand Island dressing. If you have Red Boat Salt on hand, use it generously here to season the patties and up the umami factor of the burgers even more. As you form the patties, be gentle, as overhandling the meat will result in tough and chewy burgers. You can use prepackaged ground beef, but because it has been handled multiple times before hitting the supermarket shelf, you'll gain much more flavor and texture if you pick out a nice whole chuck and ask your butcher to pass it once through the grinder instead. Alternatively, you can grind the chuck coarsely yourself at home using a food processor (briefly freezing the meat will make it easier to grind and will keep the fat intact rather than melting and smearing as the meat is processed). And while we cook the patties on our backyard grill, a scorching hot cast-iron skillet works, too.

SERVES 4

1 pound beef chuck or 80/20 ground chuck
1 scallion
¼ cup mayonnaise
¼ cup ketchup
1½ teaspoons Red Boat Fish Sauce, plus more to taste
½ small red onion
1 small tomato
Red Boat Salt or kosher salt
Ground black pepper
4 burger buns

Form the hamburger patties

1. Divide the ground beef into four equal portions and gently shape them into meatballs. Don't work or compact the meat too much—you want to work the meat just enough for it to hold its shape, and no more.
2. Place a meatball between two 6-inch square pieces of parchment. Using the palm of your hand or the bottom of a mason jar, gently press down on the meatball to form a 5½-inch patty. Repeat for the remaining meatballs.
3. Let the patties rest for at least 15 minutes. If not grilling immediately, cover and put the patties in the refrigerator until ready to grill.

Make the hamburger dressing and fixings

4. When you're ready to cook, turn the grill to medium to preheat.
5. As the grill preheats, place a dry skillet over high heat. Get it screaming hot, then add the scallion to the skillet. Roll it back and forth to char the entire exterior, about 5 minutes, then remove. When it's cool enough to handle, mince the entire scallion, green and white parts.
6. In a mixing bowl, combine the minced scallion, mayonnaise, ketchup, and fish sauce. Taste and add another dash or two of fish sauce if desired.
7. Slice the red onion into ⅛-inch-thick rings. Soak the slices in cold water for at least 15 minutes, then drain, leaving the onions in the colander or strainer over a bowl so they can continue to drain while you grill the burgers.
8. Slice the tomato into ¼-inch-thick slices. Set aside.

Grill and serve the burgers

9. Once the grill is hot, peel the top parchment paper off the patties. Mix the salt and pepper together, then season the tops of the patties with about half of the salt and pepper.
10. Place the patties on the grill, seasoned-side down. Remove the remaining sheets of parchment and sprinkle the unseasoned sides of the patties with the remaining salt and pepper.
11. Grill for 4 minutes, then flip and grill for another 4 minutes. Both sides of the patties should be browned. Transfer the patties to a platter.
12. Toast the burger buns on the grill, 30 seconds to 1 minute per side, then remove from the grill.
13. Spread the dressing on both the bottom and top buns. Add a hamburger patty to the bottom bun, then add tomatoes and onions. Top with a top bun. Serve immediately.

PAN-SEARED RIB EYES WITH RED BOAT BUTTER

Our fish sauce contains only two ingredients: black anchovies and salt. After the anchovies ferment in our barrels and have broken down into liquid, we strain the sauce, and collect the salt that's left behind—because that salt, infused with the flavors of the anchovies, is absolutely delicious. It's now one of our favorite ways to quickly add flavor to almost everything that benefits from a dry seasoning. We especially like generously sprinkling it on meats, like these rib eyes. To avoid overcooking, we sear the steaks quickly in a pan, then move them to a low-temperature oven to finish. Right before serving, we slide a thick pat of fish sauce–infused compound butter on top. This recipe does make more compound butter than you will use here, so stash the leftovers in the freezer for up to one year, or keep it in the fridge, tightly wrapped, for up to two months, for use anytime you want a richly flavored butter. You can, for instance, spread it on toast, fry an egg in it, or toss it in some fried rice.

SERVES 4

4 (¾-pound, 1-inch-thick) rib eye steaks

Red Boat Salt or kosher salt

RED BOAT BUTTER

1 pound butter, room temperature, divided

3 tablespoons minced garlic

2 tablespoons minced shallots

1 tablespoon Red Boat Fish Sauce

1 teaspoon Maggi seasoning

¼ teaspoon rice wine vinegar
Zest and juice from 1 lemon
1 tablespoon grapeseed, canola, vegetable, or other neutral oil
1 head Little Gem or butter lettuce

½ cup thinly sliced red onion

Season the steaks and make the compound butter

1. Generously season both sides of each steak with salt. Set aside at room temperature for at least 15 minutes and up to an hour.
2. Meanwhile, in a small saucepot over low heat, combine 2 tablespoons butter, garlic, and shallots. Gently cook the shallots and garlic for 15 minutes. If the aromatics start to brown, lower the heat.
3. Add the fish sauce, Maggi, and rice wine vinegar. Cook on low heat until the mixture is reduced down to about 3 tablespoons, at least 10 minutes.
4. Remove from the heat and let cool to room temperature. Add the remaining butter and lemon zest. Stir to combine.
5. Use a silicone spatula to scrape the compound butter onto the middle of an 11-inch square piece of plastic wrap. Fold the bottom end of the plastic wrap over the butter and roll the butter into a tight log. Seal the log by pinching the plastic at both ends of the roll. Twist the ends to further compact the butter into a log, then chill the compound butter in the refrigerator until firm.

Sear the rib eyes and serve

6. Preheat the oven to 250°F.
7. Coat the rib eyes with the oil. Over high heat, heat a cast-iron skillet until it's smoking hot. Working with one or two steaks at a time, add the rib eyes and sear until the bottom is browned, 2 to 3 minutes. Flip and sear the other side of the steak, then sear the edges as well. Repeat with the remaining steaks.
8. Place the steaks on a baking sheet and place in the oven to finish cooking. For medium-rare, cook to an internal temperature of 130°F (after resting, the steaks will reach 135°F).
9. Place the lettuce and onions in a mixing bowl. Add a pinch of salt and 1 teaspoon of the lemon juice and toss to coat. Divide the lettuce and onion among 4 plates.
10. Once the steaks have reached 130°F, remove them from the oven. Let the steaks rest for 5 minutes, then place each steak on a bed of lettuce and top with a generous pat of compound butter. Serve.

BÒ KHO (BEEF STEW)

This is an adaptation of my mother's bò kho recipe. Her recipes for bò kho and cà ri gà (chicken curry, page 190) are on the same page in her recipe book, and there is something so fitting about that: Both are Vietnamese classics, both comforting and homey in their own way. Where cà ri gà is a chicken-based stew, bò kho is a beefy affair, robust and hearty with a deep, glossy broth warm and fragrant with spice. My mom made this dish often, and we most often ate it with a baguette, usually bánh mì, ripping off crusty wedges and pushing them into our bowls to sop up the liquid. By the end of night, a confetti of bread crumbs blanketed the table. That's part of the fun of bò kho, but you also can serve it with rice or rice noodles if you prefer.

SERVES 4 TO 6

SPICE BLEND

- **½** teaspoon ground white pepper
- **½** teaspoon ground coriander
- **½** teaspoon ground thyme
- **1** teaspoon curry powder
- **1** tablespoon five-spice powder
- **¼** teaspoon ground paprika

BEEF

- **3** pounds rough flank, boneless short rib, or brisket, cut into 1½-inch cubes
- **2** teaspoons kosher salt
- **3** tablespoons Annatto Oil (page 287), divided

BROTH

- **3** cups 1½-inch diced white onions
- **½** cup minced lemongrass (see page 20 for tips on mincing lemongrass)
- **1** cup minced shallots
- **¼** cup minced garlic
- **1** cup sliced scallions, green tops and white parts separated

2 tablespoons minced ginger
2 tablespoons tomato paste
4 tablespoons Red Boat Fish Sauce, divided
2 star anise pods
1 small cinnamon stick
2 bay leaves
1 quart coconut water
1 tablespoon rock sugar
2 tablespoons cornstarch
3 large carrots, cut into 1-inch pieces
1 cup chopped cilantro

FOR SERVING

Bánh mì or other crusty bread, steamed rice, or cooked rice noodles

1. In a small bowl, combine all the spices in the spice blend and stir to mix well. Set aside.
2. In a large mixing bowl, add the cubed beef, salt, and 1 tablespoon of annatto oil. Mix to coat the beef in oil.
3. Place a large Dutch over high heat. When a few drops of water sprinkled into the pot evaporate immediately, the pot is ready to sear. Working in batches so you don't crowd the pot, sear the beef on all sides, then transfer to a mixing bowl and set aside.
4. To the same pot over high heat, add the remaining 2 tablespoons annatto oil. When the oil is hot, begin building the broth by first adding the diced onions. Quick-fry the onions until their edges start to brown and char in places. Use a strainer or slotted spoon to transfer the onions to a mixing bowl. Set aside.
5. Add the spice blend to the hot oil. Stir-fry the spices in the oil for about 30 seconds, then add the lemongrass, shallots, garlic, white parts of the scallions, and ginger. Sauté until aromatic, about 5 minutes. Add the tomato paste and 3 tablespoons of fish sauce. Sauté for 5 minutes, then reduce the heat to low and cook for 15 minutes, stirring every 2 minutes.
6. Tie the star anise, cinnamon stick, and bay leaves in a cheesecloth bundle and add to the pot.
7. Add the seared beef, coconut water, rock sugar, and 2 quarts water. Bring the pot to a boil. Skim off any impurities, then reduce the heat to low and simmer until the beef is tender, about 4 hours. At that point, you can remove the cheesecloth bundle.
8. Make a slurry by mixing the cornstarch with ⅓ cup water in a small bowl, then add the slurry to the pot. Add the carrots and bring the pot to a boil. Reduce the heat to low and simmer for 10 minutes.
9. Stir in the quick-fried onions, then take the pot off the heat. Taste the stew and add an additional tablespoon of fish sauce if you'd like. Garnish with the scallion tops and cilantro. Serve with crusty bread, rice, or noodles.

BRISKET PHỞ

One of my favorite spots in Sài Gòn is Phở Tàu Bay, a restaurant that's been around since 1954. I went there a lot as a kid, stopping by for a bowl of beef phở for breakfast or lunch, sometimes adding an egg that's cracked right into the hot broth to cook or a bit of extra fat to keep the bowl warm. Phở Tàu Bay has remained a destination for decades on the strength of their phở, and their continued popularity is hard-earned: It takes a considerable skill and time to make truly outstanding phở. But it is entirely possible to make excellent phở at home.

Begin the stock, as phở restaurants do, with a good mix of beef bones. Because beef bones can withstand a long simmer, many cooks pride themselves on how many days—not hours—it takes to make their stock. We keep the stock simmering with toasted spices and charred vegetables for a relatively short eight hours here, which should be enough time to break down the collagen and connective tissue on the bones that is so crucial to good phở. As you become more versed in the art of making phở, you can go longer to deepen the flavor. Serve the phở with supple noodles and thin slices of brisket, plus a generous plate of the herbs. If you really want to go the extra mile, do what I did at Phở Tàu Bay and add an egg, too. We suggest poaching it first, but you also can drop the egg directly into the bowl—just make sure your broth is hot enough to cook it!

SERVES 9

SOUP

1 (½-ounce) cinnamon stick
5 plump star anise pods
5 cloves
1 large black cardamom pod
1 pound yellow onions
2 ounces ginger, split lengthwise
4½ pounds beef bones, preferably knuckles and shank
3 pounds brisket
¼ pound daikon

2 tablespoons kosher salt
3 tablespoons granulated sugar
1 bunch scallions
¼ cup Red Boat Fish Sauce
2 pounds dry phở noodles or 3 pounds fresh phở noodles

GARNISH

1 (3-inch) segment ginger
1½ cups thinly sliced scallions
1½ cups finely chopped cilantro

FOR SERVING

Poached eggs (optional)
Bean sprouts
1 to **2** bunches Thai basil
1 to **2** bunches mint
2 limes, sliced into wedges
Serrano or Thai chiles, thinly sliced

Toast the spices and char the vegetables

1. Preheat the oven to 200°F. Wrap the cinnamon, star anise, cloves, and cardamom pod in an aluminum foil pouch. Don't wrap the pouch too tightly—the cardamom pod will expand, so be sure to leave some space for it to do so.
2. Place the pouch in the oven and toast for 15 minutes. Remove the spices from the foil pouch and tie them up in cheesecloth. Set aside.
3. Next, char the vegetables. Place a wire rack over a burner set to high heat. Place the whole onions on the rack and cook, turning the onions to char their entire exterior, for 5 to 10 minutes, depending on the strength of your range. Remove the onions to a plate.
4. Place the ginger on the rack and char the exterior, about 30 seconds. Flip the ginger and char for an additional 30 seconds. Set the ginger aside.

Make the beef stock

5. Place the bones in a pot large enough to snugly arrange them in a single layer. Add the brisket, then the charred onions and ginger, daikon, spice bundle, salt, sugar, and 3½ quarts water to the pot. (The brisket should be completely submerged in the water. If it isn't, slice the brisket into large pieces and rearrange them in the pot; you can also try rearranging the bones, or choosing a wider pot.) Over high heat, bring the water to a boil, then reduce to a very low simmer. The surface of the water should barely tremble (if you have a thermometer, the water should be about 200°F).
6. Simmer for 4 hours, then remove the brisket to a pan or large bowl. Ladle just enough of the beef stock to submerge the brisket completely. Continue simmering the large pot of stock with the bones. Place the brisket in the refrigerator to cool.
7. When the brisket has cooled, transfer it to a cutting board and pour the beef stock it was submerged in back into the pot. Slice the brisket and store it in the refrigerator until serving.

→ *continued*

8. After the beef stock has simmered for a total of 8 hours, pull up a knuckle—the collagen should easily separate from the bone. If it still clings, continue to simmer, checking every 30 minutes, until the collagen releases.

For a quicker, albeit less-complex, stock, you can make it in a pressure cooker. To do so, pressure-cook the stock for 40 minutes, then remove the brisket and plunge it into an ice bath. Slice the brisket once it's completely cool and place in the fridge until you're ready to serve. Meanwhile, continue cooking the bones for another 40 minutes, then proceed with the recipe at step 9.

9. Turn off the heat and add the bunch scallions. Steep the scallions in the stock for 1 hour, then strain the entire pot through a cloth-lined strainer. Discard the solids.
10. If using dry noodles, soak them in cold water for at least 30 minutes while the scallions steep. If using fresh noodles, skip this step.
11. Add the fish sauce to the stock. If the stock ends up being less than 3½ quarts, add enough water to make up the difference.

Assemble and serve the phở

12. Using a peeler, shave the 3-inch piece of ginger into thin sheets. Stack the sheets and slice them into very thin threads. Store in a bowl of iced water until ready to serve.
13. Bring the beef stock to a low simmer to keep warm.
14. Separately, pour 2 quarts of water into a medium pot and bring the water to a bare simmer. Place a handful of noodles into a small strainer (preferably a noodle strainer with a vertical handle). Quickly blanch the phở noodles by dunking the strainer in the simmering water for 15 seconds. Taste a noodle strand to make sure it's tender but still has bite. Shake the strainer to free any excess water, then slide the noodles into a soup bowl.
15. Add a few slices of brisket, a handful of chopped cilantro and scallions, and a pinch of ginger strands. Ladle 1½ cups beef stock over the brisket and aromatics. If you've poached any eggs, drop one in each bowl. Serve with bean sprouts, herbs, lime, and chiles.

When you make the stock, a cap of fat will form right on top. Don't throw it out! That cap contains a lot of flavor, and many phở restaurants save that fat cap and add it to their next batch of phở. You can do the same by skimming it off and freezing it. When it's time to make phở again, toss the cap in along with the brisket and charred vegetables in step 5. With every successive batch, your phở will deepen in complexity and develop its own signature flavor.

OXTAIL SOUP

Our family enjoys this meaty soup year-round, but it's especially good in the winter, when it slices through the chill in the air and warms you right up. Like many of the soups we make at home, this oxtail soup is versatile. We often modify it based on what vegetables we have in the fridge; in the summer, we switch out the kohlrabi and baby bok choy for chayote and Blue Lake beans. Feel free to use what you have on hand, or what's in season at your local farmers markets. The soup needs at least a four-hour simmer, during which time the oxtails break down and release their fat and collagen to create an exceptionally rich and full-bodied stock. If you prefer a leaner stock, chill the strained stock overnight in the fridge. The following day, skim and discard the cap of fat sitting on top, rewarm the stock, add the vegetables, and serve.

SERVES 4 TO 6

3 pounds oxtail
1 teaspoon Red Boat Salt or kosher salt
1 leek, cleaned and halved lengthwise
¼ cup Red Boat Fish Sauce
½ pound sweet onion
½ pound kohlrabi
½ pound carrots
1 pound green cabbage
¼ pound baby bok choy
2 stalks celery
½ teaspoon ground black pepper
1 teaspoon granulated sugar (optional)

→ *continued*

Prepare the oxtail stock

1. Trim the oxtail of any excess fat, reserving the trimmed fat. Season oxtail with the salt.
2. In a large Dutch oven or other heavy-bottomed pot set over high heat, sear the oxtail until all the sides are browned, approximately 4 minutes per side. Do this in small batches to avoid overcrowding the pot (crowding the pot will result in the oxtail steaming rather than searing).
3. Once all the oxtail is seared, remove the oxtail and add 1 cup of water to the pot. Use a spatula to scrape the caramelized bits stuck to the bottom of the pot. Return the oxtail to the pot.
4. Add the trimmed beef fat, leek, and an additional 3 quarts of water to the pot and bring to a boil for 15 minutes, skimming off any foam that develops.
5. Add the fish sauce, lower the heat, and simmer the stock for 4 hours. Check on the stock every so often to skim off any foam that develops on the surface.
6. While the stock cooks, prepare the vegetables: Chop the onion into ½-inch pieces, then peel and slice the kohlrabi and carrots into ¾-inch pieces. Cut the cabbage into 1-inch pieces, then quarter the baby bok choy lengthwise. Finally, using a peeler, remove the fibrous strings from the celery and slice it into ½- to 1-inch pieces. Store all the prepared vegetables in the fridge, covered, until you're ready to assemble the soup.
7. After 4 hours, fill a large bowl with water and ice. Transfer the oxtail to the ice bath and set aside.
8. Strain the stock into another large bowl. If the stock ends up being less than 2 quarts, add enough water to make up the difference.
9. Rinse out the pot, then return the strained stock to the pot along with the oxtail. If you prefer your oxtail boneless, you may remove the meat from the bones, returning only the meat to the stock.

Make the soup

10. Bring the stock to a boil, then add the onions, kohlrabi, carrots, and celery. Cook for approximately 15 minutes, skimming off any foam that develops.
11. Add the cabbage and baby bok choy and cook for 3 to 5 minutes, then take the pot off the heat.
12. Season the soup with black pepper and taste. If you'd like the soup to be a little sweeter, add the sugar.
13. Ladle the soup into bowls and serve steaming hot.

To save time, the stock can also be made with a pressure cooker. After searing the oxtail in step 3, transfer the oxtail and its liquid to the pressure cooker. Add 3 cups of water, then cover and set for 45 minutes of high pressure. While the stock cooks, prepare the vegetables according to step 6. After 45 minutes, allow the pot to depressure naturally, then remove the oxtail to the ice bath, strain the stock, and continue with the recipe at step 9.

CHRISTINE HÀ'S LAAB (THAI MINCED PORK SALAD)

When Christine Hà won *MasterChef* in 2012, I was so happy for her, and, honestly, quite emotional, as were many other Vietnamese and Vietnamese Americans. It was significant moment for Vietnamese representation on American television; even now, almost ten years later, I still remember the dish she made in that final round of competition: thịt kho, braised and caramelized pork belly, a staple of Vietnamese home cooking, and the one dish that exemplifies home for so many of us. In 2019, she opened a gastropub, The Blind Goat, and her second spot, Xin Chào, in 2020, both in Houston. We're excited to continue supporting her and her wonderful cooking. Although she is mostly known for Vietnamese cooking, she also makes a terrific laab, a minced meat salad that has variations throughout Laos and Thailand. The ground meat is dressed in lime juice and fish sauce, with chiles and herbs tossed in right at the end. The result is a refreshing salad that is savory, tangy, and spicy all at once. We use ground beef here, but you can also use ground chicken, turkey, or pork.

SERVES 4

2 pounds ground beef
2 limes, juiced and divided
6 tablespoons Red Boat Fish Sauce, divided
1 shallot, thinly sliced
4 scallions, thinly sliced
1 to **2** Thai red chile peppers, seeded if desired and minced, or ½ tablespoon red chile flakes
¼ cup chopped Thai basil
¼ cup chopped cilantro
2 tablespoons chopped mint

GARNISH

¼ cup roasted peanuts, chopped
2 to **4** tablespoons toasted rice (optional)

FOR SERVING

Jasmine rice
Butter lettuce leaves

1. In a medium bowl, mix together the ground meat, juice of 1 lime, and 3 tablespoons of fish sauce and let stand for 10 minutes.
2. In a sauté pan over medium-high heat, cook the meat until browned. Transfer the meat to a large bowl, reserving the rendered fat in the pan and draining any excess liquid.
3. Add the shallot and scallions to the pan and sauté until fragrant, just a minute, then fold in the meat. Add the remaining 3 tablespoons of fish sauce, the juice of the second lime, chile peppers, basil, cilantro, and mint.
4. Garnish with roasted peanuts and toasted rice if using. Serve with rice and lettuce leaves for wrapping.

CHAPTER 8

Every holiday or special occasion in our house is cause for a big feast: a big pot of pork belly braised in a caramel sauce simmering on the stove, a platter of xôi thập cẩm (sticky rice with chicken, Chinese sausage, and shallots) on the table, the refrigerator jammed full of pickles and nước chấm, a cooler of drinks for the kids and the adults. And, of course, family and friends gathered around, filling and refilling and refilling their plates.

When I was a kid in Việt Nam, the holidays were always a happy time, especially because everyone always eventually ended up at our house, or at least came by to pick up food. This probably isn't a surprise: My mother was well known for her cooking, and for the holidays she spent days carefully planning and preparing, enlisting my sister's help in the kitchen to have everything ready for the feast. Her mooncakes were legendary; family lore has it that every year, she had to order one thousand eggs—one thousand!—to accommodate all the orders she received during the Mid-Autumn Moon Festival.

And while everything she made was always just right for that occasion, there were two holidays in particular where she really manifested her culinary prowess: đám giỗ and Tết.

Đám giỗ is the anniversary of an ancestor's death. Every family has their own way of celebrating the anniversary, but it's generally a time to express gratitude and filial piety, and to honor the memory of the departed. For many Vietnamese families who have experienced separation through multiple eras of unrest and war, the anniversary is especially poignant.

Đám giỗ can be a multiday affair, with friends and former colleagues invited to pay their respects to the dead. Food is a huge part of đám giỗ; along with classic feasting dishes like egg rolls, the honoree's favorite foods are also prepared. For every đám giỗ after my grandfather passed, my mother prepared all his favorites: cháo bồi (a silky rice porridge dressed up with tapioca pearls and mushrooms, page 218), a lotus root salad (page 223), and thịt kho (braised and caramelized pork belly, page 229). Just one look at all those dishes on the table, and you knew instantly the đám giỗ was for him. There was more than enough for everyone, including grandpa; we'd place bowls of porridge and thịt kho on his altar before serving ourselves.

As it happens, my grandfather's đám giỗ occurs right around

another major holiday in our family: Tết. Now, Tết does not feel like Tết without a pot of my mother's special thịt kho (braised pork belly), with its generous slabs of pork belly and a braising liquid that includes coconut water; that thịt kho always did double duty as it transitioned from its role at the đám giỗ to its role during Tết. We also had stacks of bánh chưng—rice cakes wrapped in banana leaves—on the table, some gifted to us, some ready to be gifted to others.

We continued these traditions when we immigrated to the United States, with my mother spearheading the cooking during all the holidays. She was also the Vietnamese equivalent of the Butterball hotline: If she wasn't tending to the stove or at the counter rolling out dough, she was on the phone with friends or extended family, fielding questions about how to cook this or troubleshoot that. She did it all.

Since both my parents passed, we've met at my sister's place to celebrate holidays, anniversaries, and other special days. The dishes we make for these special occasions are the dishes we feature in this chapter. Some are very special dishes we generally make only for special days, as they're involved and take a bit of time to shop for, prepare, and cook. But there are also a few dishes, like xôi, which is a treat during Tết as well as throughout the year. Taken together, these are all dishes fit for a Phamily feast, whatever the occasion.

CHÁO BỒI (BROKEN RICE AND TAPIOCA PORRIDGE)

To this day, I associate cháo bồi with my mother and all the times she made it for her dad, including every year for his đám giỗ, or anniversary of his death. It takes a little bit of time to prepare all the ingredients for this silky, delicate porridge brimming with fresh shrimp and crab, but for any special occasion, it's worth the time. Because it relies on so few ingredients, quality definitely matters, particularly the quality of the seafood. My mom was fortunate to have ready access to fresh fish and shellfish; if possible, pick up fresh crab and shrimp from your local fishmonger or market (we often buy whole, steamed crabs at Costco or our local Asian market and remove the meat ourselves at home). If fresh crab meat is unavailable, substitute quality oysters, abalone, or additional fresh shrimp. You can buy bags of broken rice at your local Asian grocer, or you can soak whole rice grains in water for 30 minutes, then break them up with your hands. Tapioca pearls give the bowl a bit of body without making the porridge starchy. Packages of tapioca pearls can also be found at major Asian markets.

→ *continued*

SERVES 6 TO 8

1 pound pork loin or leg
1½ tablespoons plus **1** teaspoon kosher salt, divided
¾ cup broken rice (see page 22)
3 tablespoons dried small tapioca pearls or sago
1 ounce dried shredded wood ear mushrooms
1 teaspoon baking soda
½ pound shrimp, peeled and deveined
Ground black pepper
¼ cup plus **½** teaspoon Red Boat Fish Sauce, divided, plus additional to taste
½ pound crab meat, from about 2 pounds of freshly steamed whole crabs

GARNISH

Fried Shallots (page 290), homemade or store-bought
1 cup chopped scallions
½ bunch cilantro, chopped
1 lime, cut into wedges

Make the broth

1. In a 5-quart pot, bring 2 quarts of water to a boil. Add the pork leg and 1 teaspoon salt and boil for 3 to 4 minutes to remove the impurities from the pork.
2. Remove the leg and set aside. Drain and rinse the pot, then refill it with 3 quarts of water. Over medium heat, bring the water to a boil and place the pork back into the pot. Reduce the heat to a simmer and cook until the pork is tender, about 50 minutes.
3. Transfer the pork to a bowl filled with ice and water. Let cool completely.
4. Skim any foam or impurities from the simmering broth. Set aside.

Make the porridge

5. Rinse the broken rice until the water runs clear. Add the rice to the pork broth, bring it to a boil, then reduce to a simmer. Cook until the rice kernels are tender and almost break down, 50 to 60 minutes, stirring frequently so the rice doesn't stick to the pot. Adjust the heat as necessary to keep the broth at a bare simmer.

While the porridge cooks, prepare the fillings

6. **TAPIOCA PEARLS:** Rinse the tapioca pearls three times in water, then soak in 1 quart cold water. Set aside.

7. **MUSHROOMS:** Rehydrate the dried mushrooms by soaking in 1 quart of warm water, stirring them around in the water to loosen any grit. When the mushrooms have completely rehydrated, about 20 minutes, drain in a colander and roughly chop. Set aside.
8. **SHRIMP:** In a medium mixing bowl, dissolve the baking soda and remaining 1½ tablespoons salt in 2 cups water. Add the shrimp and let it sit in the brine in the refrigerator for 15 to 30 minutes. Drain the shrimp, then dry between paper towels.
9. Add the shrimp, a pinch of black pepper, and ½ teaspoon fish sauce to a food processor and process to a smooth paste. Transfer to a mixing bowl and marinate in the refrigerator until needed.
10. **PORK:** Carve the pork leg into ¼-inch slices, then cut into strips. Set aside.

Add the fillings to the porridge

11. When the rice kernels reach the desired texture, drain the tapioca pearls and add them and the wood ear mushrooms to the pot. Simmer the pearls in the porridge until they are translucent, about 15 minutes.
12. Scoop out ½ tablespoon of shrimp paste and drop it into the porridge. Repeat with the remainder of the paste. Add ¼ cup of fish sauce. Give the porridge a few gentle stirs and simmer over low heat for an additional 5 to 7 minutes, until the shrimp is firm and opaque all the way through. Taste. If you'd like, add an additional splash or two of fish sauce.
13. Take the pot off heat. Add the shredded pork and crab meat.
14. Ladle the porridge into serving bowls. Garnish with fried shallots, chopped scallions, and cilantro. Serve hot, with lime wedges for the table.

VIETNAMESE LOTUS ROOT SALAD

Đám giỗ, the anniversary of a loved one's death, is about as big of a deal as a birthday. It's a festive time, with a lot of cooking and fond reminiscing. One of our must-have dishes for the occasion is this crisp lotus root salad that's a favorite of many southern Vietnamese families. As with many holiday foods, this salad has several components and takes a bit of prep to pull together. Indeed, as my sister tells it, our mother would always start this salad first thing in the morning. She would wake up extra early, organize the ingredients, thinly slice all the vegetables by hand, then prepare the dressing. She also fried prawn crackers, a more flavorful version of shrimp chips that puff up beautifully in hot oil (the crackers are usually packaged in boxes and can be picked up at Asian markets, along with everything else you'll need for this salad). It was a lot of work, but every step was done with enormous care—that's just who my mom was. Then, when it was time to serve, all she had to do was mix everything together. You can do the same. If you don't have any rau răm in your fridge, you can replace it with an equal amount of mint.

→ *continued*

SERVES 6

SALAD

1 medium red onion

3 cucumbers, preferably Persian or Japanese varieties, quartered, seeds removed, and cut into matchsticks

Kosher salt

1 (24-ounce) jar pickled lotus rootlets

2 pounds pork tenderloin

2 pounds large (16/20) shell-on shrimp

8 stalks celery, peeled and cut into matchsticks

½ pound carrots, peeled and cut into matchsticks

1 cup loosely packed rau răm, coarsely chopped

4 cups loosely packed mint, coarsely chopped

DRESSING

6 Thai chiles, stem and seeds removed, minced

¼ cup lime juice

¼ cup plus **2** tablespoons lemon juice

1 tablespoon minced garlic

¾ cup granulated sugar

½ cup Red Boat Fish Sauce

GARNISH

2 cups oven-roasted unsalted peanuts, chopped

Fried Shallots (page 290), or store-bought

16 prawn crackers, prepared according to package instructions

Prepare the vegetables, shrimp, and pork

1. Halve the onion lengthwise, cutting through the root end. Soak the halves in water for 30 minutes to mellow out the harshness, then thinly slice each half and set aside.
2. Place the cucumbers in a small bowl and toss with ¼ teaspoon of kosher salt. Set aside for 30 minutes to allow the salt to draw out the excess moisture from the cucumbers. After 30 minutes, gently squeeze the cucumbers to remove any excess moisture, then let them drain in a colander. Set aside.
3. Drain the lotus rootlets and slice them lengthwise into halves, then quarters. Transfer the rootlets to a large bowl. Add 2 quarts of water and soak for 10 minutes. Drain, and soak them again in 2 quarts of fresh water for another 10 minutes. Drain the rootlets, squeezing them to remove any excess water: You want the rootlets to be as dry as possible for the salad. Transfer the rootlets to a colander set in a bowl and set aside.
4. Cut the pork into 6-inch-long pieces and place the pieces in a medium-size pot set over high heat. Add 1 teaspoon of salt and enough water to cover the pork. As the pot heats, prepare an ice bath by filling a large bowl with ice and water. When the pot comes to a boil, reduce the heat to a

bare simmer. Poach the meat until its internal temperature reaches 145°F for medium-rare and 160°F for medium. Transfer the pieces to the prepared ice bath to stop the cooking. When the pieces are cool enough to handle, slice them into thin strips.

5. Fill another large bowl with water and ice and set aside. Peel and devein the shrimp. In a medium pot, bring 1 quart of water to a boil. Carefully add the shrimp, then reduce the water to a bare simmer. Poach the shrimp until their centers are completely opaque, about 5 minutes, then plunge them in the ice bath. When they've cooled, remove them from the bath and slice in half lengthwise. Set aside.

Shell-on shrimp is preferable to pre-peeled shrimp because they usually are fresher. And save those shells! Place them in a resealable freezer bag and store them in your freezer. When you have enough, use them to make Buttery Shellfish Stock, page 297.

Make the dressing, assemble the salad, and serve

6. Place the minced Thai chiles in a glass jar. Add the lime juice, lemon juice, garlic, sugar, and fish sauce and whisk well to combine. If not using immediately, refrigerate the dressing until serving, up to 3 days in advance.

7. In a large mixing bowl, combine the onions, cucumbers, lotus rootlets, pork, shrimp, celery, carrots, rau răm, and mint. Pour the dressing on top and mix well (it's best to use your hands to massage the dressing into the vegetables, but you can also use tongs if you prefer). Transfer the salad to a serving bowl. Sprinkle peanuts and fried shallots on top. Serve with prawn chips.

XÔI THẬP CẨM

(STICKY RICE WITH CHICKEN, LẠP XƯỞNG, AND SHALLOTS)

No matter the holiday or special occasion, xôi is always, always part of the feast. Made with sticky rice, xôi's special role in every festivity and holiday harkens back to the days when glutinous rice required considerably more labor and expense to make and obtain than nonsticky rice. These days, harvesting glutinous rice still requires much effort, but it is more widely available; satchels can be found at most markets, and a rice cooker with a sticky or sweet rice setting will cook the rice in no time, so xôi has become a dish we make even outside of the holidays. Here's one of our favorite versions, where chicken, lạp xưởng (also known as Chinese sausage), and pork floss are gently folded into the sticky rice and finished with a shower of fried shallots right on top. We can eat this xôi any time of the day, from breakfast to lunch to dinner, or as a snack in between. And, of course, it is a must-have during the holidays.

SERVES 4 TO 6

2 cups sweet rice, soaked for 2 hours, then drained

4 skin-on boneless chicken thighs

2 tablespoons olive oil, divided

1 teaspoon Red Boat Fish Sauce or **¼** teaspoon Red Boat Salt

¼ teaspoon ground black pepper

¼ pound lạp xưởng (see page 20)

¼ cup minced shallots or ⅓ minced white onion

1 teaspoon Maggi seasoning

2 tablespoons Red Boat Scallion Oil (page 285), plus additional for serving

Thịt chà bông (also known as ruốc, rousong, and pork floss) (optional)

2 cups Fried Shallots (page 290), or store-bought

1. **RICE COOKER METHOD:** Place the rice in the rice cooker's bowl and rinse several times until the water runs clear. Add ⅔ cup of water and cook the rice in your rice cooker using the sweet rice setting.

You can also use ⅔ cup of chicken stock (page 292 or store-bought), instead of water to cook the rice in the rice cooker.

   STEAMER BASKET METHOD: Rinse the rice several times until the water runs clear. Line the bottom of a steamer basket with a clean cloth, like a bandana, then spread the rice in one even layer on the cloth. Add ⅔ cup of water to the pot and steam the rice, covered, stirring occasionally to fluff up the rice, for 1 hour.
2. Preheat the oven to 350°F.
3. Place the chicken thighs in a roasting pan with 1 tablespoon of oil. Coat the chicken with the oil, then season with fish sauce (or Red Boat Salt) and black pepper. Marinate the chicken for at least 15 minutes and up to 8 hours in the fridge.
4. Position the thighs skin-side up. Roast for 30 minutes, then remove the roasting pan from the oven and place on a cooling rack to cool.
5. Line a large plate with paper towels. Slice the lạp xưởng thinly on a bias. In a medium-size pan over medium heat, pan-fry the lạp xưởng (the fat will render as the sausage is heated, so there's no need to add any oil to the pan first). Cook, stirring the slices, just until they begin to curl slightly, about 5 minutes. Do not brown. Transfer the lạp xưởng onto the paper towel–lined plate to drain.
6. Use another paper towel to wipe the pan clean, then place the pan over medium-low heat. Add the remaining 1 tablespoon olive oil to the pan, then add the shallots or onion. Cook until translucent and browned, just a few minutes, then remove from the pan and set aside.
7. When the chicken is cool enough to handle, transfer it to a bowl, leaving the drippings in the pan. Shred the thighs using a fork or your hands and set aside. Add the Maggi to the pan drippings.
8. When the rice finishes cooking, transfer to a large bowl, sprinkle the drippings onto the rice, and mix it well to coat the grains. Add the shredded chicken, lạp xưởng, and sautéed shallots (or onion) to the rice and mix gently to incorporate the ingredients.
9. Transfer the sticky rice to a serving platter, drizzle with the scallion oil, then top with a handful of thịt chà bông, if using, and fried shallots. Serve hot or at room temperature, along with extra scallion oil for guests to add as they wish.

HOLIDAY THỊT KHO TRỨNG (EXTRA-SPECIAL CARAMELIZED PORK FOR THE LUNAR NEW YEAR)

When I think of my mother, I think of this dish, especially during Tết, the Lunar New Year. The celebration goes on for at least a week, with the first few days reserved for spending time with family without the distraction of work or even turning on the stove. With restaurants across the country closed for the holiday, it pays to have a big batch of something made in advance that you can reheat for a crowd. For us and so many other Vietnamese and Vietnamese Americans, Tết isn't Tết without a bowl (or two, or three) of a beloved holiday kho with generous pieces of skin-on belly. For a leaner kho, you can replace half the belly with pork shoulder.

→ *continued*

SERVES 4

2 pounds skin-on pork belly, sliced into large pieces
1 teaspoon kosher salt
⅓ to **½** cup Red Boat Fish Sauce

1 (12-ounce) can coconut soda, or 16 ounces coconut water plus **1** to **2** tablespoons granulated sugar, to taste
6 hard-boiled eggs

FOR SERVING
Steamed rice
2 cucumbers, sliced

1. Place the pork in a medium pot with enough water to cover the meat by 1 inch, about 2 quarts. Add the salt. Boil for 10 minutes to remove the impurities from the pork, then drain and rinse the meat, scrubbing each piece to remove any remaining impurities.
2. Transfer the pork back to the pot and place over medium heat. Add ⅓ cup of fish sauce and the coconut soda (or the coconut water plus 1 tablespoon of sugar), cover, and reduce the heat to simmer.
3. After about 30 minutes, the pork will begin to brown. At that point, add enough water to cover the pork by 1 inch, and stir. Continue simmering, partially uncovered, for 1½ to 2 hours, or until the pork is tender and cooked through.
4. Add the hardboiled eggs and continue simmering for 10 minutes. Taste for seasoning: Add additional fish sauce or sugar if needed; you can also add more water if you'd like the liquid to be a little looser. Serve with steamed rice and cucumbers.

TIP

The thịt will taste even better the next day and the day after that. To save your leftovers, place everything in an airtight container and refrigerate for up to 3 days.

LẨU (SHRIMP HOT POT)

My sister Điệp makes this beautiful soup on holidays like Tết, the Lunar New Year, and it truly is a soup you make on special occasions for loved family and friends. It's the sum of lẩu's many components that make it so special: a homemade pork stock; freshly made shrimp paste stuffed into mushroom caps and rolled into egg spirals; and, finally, a variety of fresh vegetables, including carrots that we take the time to carve into decorative shapes. Even with these multiple parts, the soup is light and restorative—a nice respite from the richness of the other holiday dishes.

SERVES 4 TO 6

3 tablespoons kosher salt
2 teaspoons baking soda
1 pound whole shrimp, peeled, deveined, and thoroughly dried with a paper towel
1 teaspoon Red Boat Fish Sauce
1 teaspoon granulated sugar
1 tablespoon minced garlic
3 eggs
Vegetable oil or butter, for greasing the pan
6 to **8** shiitake mushrooms, caps only
2 large carrots
1½ quarts Pork Stock (page 294)
¼ head of a large cauliflower or **½** head of a small cauliflower, cut into florets
½ small napa cabbage, chopped
2 cups yu choy, bok choy, pea tendrils, or other leafy green, chopped into approximately 2-inch-long pieces
½ cup pork cracklings, broken into bite-size pieces

Make the shrimp paste

1. In a medium mixing bowl, dissolve the salt and baking soda in 2 cups water. Add the shrimp and let it sit in the brine in the refrigerator for 15 to 30 minutes. Drain the shrimp, then dry between paper towels.

→ *continued*

2. Add the shrimp, fish sauce, sugar, and garlic to a food processor. Process the shrimp to a smooth paste. Transfer the shrimp paste to a mixing bowl and marinate in the refrigerator for 2 to 3 hours.

Make and fill the omelets and mushrooms

3. Crack the eggs into a bowl and beat well.
4. Heat a teaspoon of oil in an 8-inch sauté pan set over low heat. When the oil shimmers, ladle ¼ cup beaten egg into the pan. Gently tilt the pan to distribute the eggs into an even, thin omelet. Let the eggs cook undisturbed until set, about 1 minute. Turn the omelet onto a plate or cutting board. Repeat with the remainder of the beaten eggs.
5. Working with one omelet at a time, place about 3 tablespoons of the shrimp paste in the omelet's center. Using a butter knife, spread the paste across the surface to create one thin, even layer, adding more shrimp paste if necessary. Tightly roll the omelet and set aside. Repeat with the remaining omelets.
6. Flip the mushroom caps over and spread about 1 tablespoon of the shrimp paste on the underside of each cap.
7. Fill a pot fitted with a large steamer basket with about 2 inches of water and set over medium heat. When the water begins to boil, place the omelet rolls and mushroom caps in the steam basket, cover, and steam until the shrimp is completely cooked, about 10 minutes.
8. Remove the mushrooms and omelet rolls from the steamer basket, then carefully slice the omelets crosswise into ¼-inch pieces. Set aside.

Finish the soup

9. Discard the stem ends and tips of the carrots, then slice them lengthwise into ¼-inch-thick strips. Cut the strips into 1½-inch pieces.

   Alternatively, create star-shaped slices: Working with one carrot at a time, hold a sharp knife at a 45-degree angle along the length of the carrot and make a cut about ⅛-inch deep. Angle the knife 45 degrees in the opposite direction of the first cut, and slice about ⅛ inch lengthwise down the carrot. Remove the resulting V-shaped wedge, then rotate the carrot 90 degrees and make the same two cuts. Repeat twice more around the carrot, then slice the carrot crosswise into ¼-inch pieces. Repeat for the second carrot. Set aside.
10. Heat the pork stock in a large pot set over medium heat. When the stock is at a strong simmer, add the carrots and cauliflower. Reduce the heat to low and gently simmer until the vegetables are tender, about 10 minutes.
11. Drop the napa leaves and leafy greens into the stock for 1 minute, or just long enough to warm them. Turn off the heat.
12. To serve, ladle the soup and vegetables into serving bowls. Top with the sliced omelet rolls, mushroom caps, and pork cracklings.

LI'L BÁNH CHƯNG

(LUNAR NEW YEAR RICE CAKES FILLED WITH PORK, MUNG BEANS, AND SHALLOTS)

Lunar New Year cakes come in a variety of shapes. The southern-style bánh tét is cylindrical, for example, and the northern-style bánh chưng is square. Both, however, generally have the same savory ingredients that complement each other well: rich pork, buttery mung beans, and sweet shallots. And both tend to be enormous in size, as they're meant to be gifted, something you present to relatives and friends as you make your Tết rounds. The size is a reflection of the gifter's largess and affection for the giftee.

The northern-style recipe we have here comes courtesy our R&D chef, Diep Tran, who founded the Bánh Chưng Collective. Every Lunar New Year, the collective organizes communal bánh chưng–making sessions across the country, guiding participants as they make stacks of single-size portions of bánh chưng. These li'l bánh chưng offer a few advantages over their larger cousins. For one thing, the ratio of pork and mung beans to rice is higher, creating a more flavorful bánh chưng.

In addition, their small size means they'll take less time to cook—you can even cook them in an Instant Pot, as the Bánh Chưng Collective does at their events, but if you don't have an Instant Pot or pressure cooker, we also include instructions on how to cook your bánh chưng on the stovetop. To gift these, Diep suggests demonstrating your generosity by bundling eight bánh chưng together to recreate the size of the big cakes.

→ *continued*

To make the bánh chưng, you will need twine and a 3 x 3 x 2-inch mold. We use molds from the brand Ateco, which can be purchased online or at baking supply stores; you can also fashion your own mold if you're handy with carpentry or a 3D printer. Fresh banana leaves, a must for wrapping the bánh chưng, can be purchased at Latin American markets, particularly those servicing Salvadoran and Guatemalan communities.

MAKES 16 BÁNH CHƯNG

2 pounds pork belly
½ cup Red Boat Fish Sauce, divided
1 teaspoon black pepper, divided
2 pounds sweet rice
1 pound mung beans
1 stick (½ cup) butter
4 shallots, diced
2 pounds fresh banana leaves

Day 1: Marinate the pork and soak the rice and mung beans

1. Slice the pork belly into 1½-inch squares that are about ⅓ inch thick. Place the slices in a bowl with 4 teaspoons of fish sauce and ½ teaspoon black pepper. Stir to coat the slices with the fish sauce and pepper, then place in the refrigerator to marinate overnight.
2. Soak the sweet rice and mung beans in separate bowls of water (both will expand while they soak, so be sure to use a generous amount of water). Place both bowls in the refrigerator to soak overnight.

Day 2: Prepare the filling

3. Drain the mung beans and rinse through two changes of water. Repeat for the rice.
4. Transfer the mung beans to a medium pot. Add 3 quarts of water and bring the beans to a boil.
5. Reduce the heat and simmer until they're tender, but not falling apart, about 10 minutes. Set a colander in the sink and drain the mung beans. Let cool.
6. Add the butter to a sauté pan. Over medium heat, melt the butter until it foams. Add the shallots and sauté for a minute, then reduce the heat to low. Cook the shallots until they caramelize and break down, about 10 minutes.

7. Take the pan off the heat and add the remaining scant ½ cup fish sauce and ½ teaspoon black pepper. Stir to combine.
8. Add the drained mung beans to the pan. Stir until the mung beans and shallots are evenly distributed throughout the filling. Transfer to a bowl and set aside to cool.

Create a banana leaf box

9. Stack six strips of banana leaves horizontally in the middle of your work surface. Place the mold in the center of the strips. Fold the left side of the strips up against the side of the mold.
10. Set aside the banana leaves and return the mold to the middle of your work surface.
11. Insert one strip inside the mold, with the folded edge flush against the left wall of the mold. Make a corresponding fold that is flush against the right wall of the mold. Take a second strip and place it perpendicular to the first, making folds against the top and bottom walls of the mold. Repeat with the third and fourth strips. Alternating the direction of the grain with each layer of strips in this way will create a strong structure to cook the bánh chưng.

For a bánh chưng with neat, crisp edges, make sure that your folds are sharp!

12. Now that you have created a strong base for the box, reinforce the side walls by lining the perimeter with the remaining two strips, trimming as necessary to fit.
13. Trim the other excess strips, leaving an overhang of 2½ inches. You'll end up with a box shape that's ready to hold the bánh chưng ingredients.

Add the filling

14. For a uniform bánh chưng that doesn't fall apart when it cooks, surround the pork and mung bean with plenty of the sweet rice to prevent the filling from touching the sides of your banana leaf box. To start, place 3 tablespoons of rice into the mold, tamping down the rice so it settles into an even layer at the bottom, then build the rice up along the sides. Add a slice of pork belly and 1 tablespoon mung beans in the center in the rice bed. Add about an additional 2 tablespoons of sweet rice to fill in the rest of the mold, making sure the rice fills in the gap between the sides of the box and the pork and mung bean. Press down on the rice. If any mung beans show through, add more rice to cover. The rice should be level with the lip of the mold.
15. Fold over the overhanging strips of banana leaves to close the box, pressing down to compact the ingredients. Place a piece of twine on top of the box. Flip the packet over and carefully remove the mold. Use the twine to bind the banana leaf box together. Set aside and repeat with remaining ingredients.

Cook the bánh chưng

16. You can cook the bánh chưng in a pressure cooker or on the stove.

PRESSURE COOKER METHOD: Place the bánh chưng in your pressure cooker, and add water until it reaches the top of the highest bánh chưng. Pressure cook the bánh chưng for 50 minutes.

STOVE TOP METHOD: Arrange the bánh chưng in a large stockpot and fill the pot with water, making sure the bánh chưng is submerged in at least 4 inches of water. Over high heat, bring the pot to a boil, then reduce the heat and simmer for 7 hours.

17. Transfer the cooked bánh chưng onto a wire rack–lined baking sheet to cool for 5 minutes. Once the bánh chưng is cool enough to handle, rinse them under water and wipe off the boiling liquid. Transfer the bánh chưng back onto the wire rack to drain.

18. Unwrap the bánh chưng and discard the banana leaves right before serving.

DEEP FRIED BÁNH CHƯNG:

Bánh chưng can be enjoyed at room temperature, and warm, fresh bánh chưng is heavenly and needs no adornment. Deep-fried bánh chưng with its crisp crust, topped with Scallion Oil (page 285) is a whole other thing altogether. For deep-fried bánh chưng, chill the bánh chưng in the refrigerator for at least 2 hours, then remove the banana leaves and place the bánh chưng onto a wire-lined baking sheet. Dry out the bánh chưng in the refrigerator for another 2 to 4 hours. Fry the bánh chưng in 325°F oil until the exterior is crisp and golden.

RED BOAT HOLIDAY TURKEY WITH GRAVY

This is the turkey our R&D chef, Diep Tran, originally developed for her restaurant, Good Girl Dinette, and she continues to make this turkey every year. To achieve a juicy, richly flavored holiday turkey, Diep takes the initial step of spatchcocking the bird so it lays it flat while roasting (if you'd rather not do this step yourself, it's worth asking if your butcher could do it for you). The advantage of this method is it reduces the oven time and ensures the turkey roasts evenly. She then slathers the bird with a wet rub of ginger, toasted spices, and Red Boat Fish Sauce and lets it sit in the fridge for up to four days. Finally, when it's time to roast, Diep encases the turkey in generously buttered parchment paper to keep the bird juicy and tender. The inspiration for this technique, she says, came after reading a 1995 *Saveur* article about the Southern cook Anne Scott Coleman and her mother, LouElla Hill, who roasted her turkey in a buttered paper bag. While the turkey roasts, Diep prepares a delicious gravy, using the backbone removed from spatchcocking the bird to build the stock. The gravy is finished with a few spoonfuls of fish sauce swirled in right before serving.

SERVES 8 TO 10

1 (12-pound) turkey

MARINADE

7 cloves

2 tablespoons ground coriander, preferably freshly ground

¼ cup minced ginger

2 sticks (1 cup) butter, divided

7 cloves garlic

→ *continued*

1 medium white onion, diced
¼ cup granulated sugar
1 bunch scallions, sliced into 2-inch pieces, green and white parts
½ cup Red Boat Fish Sauce
3 tablespoons ground black pepper

GRAVY
¾ pound white or yellow onion, chopped
2 stalks celery, chopped
¼ cup (½ stick) unsalted butter
1 tablespoon all-purpose flour
2 cups heavy cream
3 tablespoons Red Boat Fish Sauce
1 teaspoon ground black pepper

Spatchcock the turkey

1. Position the turkey with the breast side facing down. Using heavy-duty culinary shears, cut down both sides of the backbone. Remove the backbone and save for making the gravy.
2. With the breast side still facing down, use a heavy-duty knife to cut through the middle of the wishbone.
3. Turn the turkey breast-side up. Push down the breast with both hands until the breastbone cracks and the turkey lies flat.
4. Place the turkey on a baking sheet fitted with a wire rack and place in the refrigerator while you make the marinade.

Make the marinade

5. Grind the cloves into a fine powder.
6. In a small pan over medium heat, fry the ground cloves, ground coriander, and ginger in 1 stick of butter until the coriander powder begins to darken and the ginger starts to caramelize.
7. Add the garlic and onion and fry until fragrant, about 2 minutes.
8. Transfer the onion mixture to the bowl of a food processor. Add the sugar and scallions, then process until the ginger in the mixture is finely ground.
9. Transfer the mixture to a bowl. Add the fish sauce and black pepper and stir to combine.
10. Take the baking sheet with the turkey out of the refrigerator. Rub the mixture on both the skin and underside of the turkey. Marinate for at least 1 day—ideally 4 days—in the refrigerator.

Roast the turkey

11. When you're ready to roast the turkey, preheat the oven to 375°F.
12. Remove the turkey from the refrigerator. Take a piece of parchment paper large enough to cover the entire turkey and rub one side with an entire stick of butter. Place the parchment paper, butter-side down, over the turkey, tucking the parchment paper under the rack so there's no overhang.
13. Roast the turkey. After 1 hour, remove the parchment paper and

rotate the turkey. Continue roasting, rotating the turkey every 20 minutes to ensure even browning. The turkey is done once its internal temperature reaches 165°F, or about an hour after you first rotate the bird.

14. Remove the turkey from the oven and let it rest in the baking sheet for 20 minutes. Transfer to a serving platter, saving the drippings that have collected on the baking sheet to make the gravy.

Make the gravy

15. Start the gravy by making a turkey stock: Place the turkey backbone, turkey neck, onion, celery, and enough water to cover in a medium pot over high heat. Bring to a boil, then reduce to a simmer and cook for 2½ hours. Strain and set aside.

    Alternatively, you can make the stock in a pressure cooker if you have one: Place the backbone, turkey neck, onions, celery, and enough water to cover in the pressure cooker. Cook for 20 minutes, then strain and set aside.

16. Meanwhile, deglaze the baking sheet: Pour the turkey drippings in the baking sheet into a cup. Skim and discard the fat, leaving the remaining juices in the cup. Set the baking sheet over medium heat and pour in 1 cup of water. Working quickly with a spatula, deglaze the sheet by scraping up the bits of caramelized juice sticking to the pan. Carefully pour the liquid into the cup with the drippings and set aside.

17. Make a roux: Place the butter and flour in a medium sauce pot over medium heat. Stirring continuously, cook until the mixture turns a deep golden color, being sure to work out any lumps in the roux. A smooth roux will result in a smooth gravy.

18. Add the drippings and deglazing liquid to the pot and bring to a boil, then add 1½ cups of the turkey stock. Bring it to a boil, then add the heavy cream and again bring to a boil. Continue boiling until the gravy has reduced and is thick enough to coat the back of a spoon.

19. Add 1 tablespoon of fish sauce. Taste and add up to 2 more tablespoons of fish sauce if needed. If the sauce is too salty, add more turkey stock. Transfer the gravy to a serving bowl or gravy boat and serve with the turkey.

Save and use the turkey bones for stock. To do so, use the same techniques for making chicken stock (page 292). That turkey stock is perfect for making an invigorating bowl of porridge (page 38) the morning after this feast. And any leftover turkey meat will be a great filling in a bánh mì. See page 34 for tips on building your own bánh mì.

CHAPTER 9

SWEETS & DRINKS

MANGO STICKY RICE WITH COCONUT CREAM SAUCE

After a session of testing and tasting our fish sauce at the barrel house, we often break for a platter of sliced mangoes, letting the fruit's sweetness cut through the salt lingering on our palates. Similarly, fresh mangoes are a great way to end a rich meal. You can do as we do at the barrel house and serve them simply sliced, maybe with a sprinkle of chile flakes, or you can prepare our take on the classic mango sticky rice. Our version adds a bit of our palm sugar and Red Boat Salt to the coconut cream before it's spooned over the dessert; the two complement the fruit and sticky rice so well that you'll want to keep a ramekins of them handy for when your guests ask for more.

SERVES 2

2 cups sweet rice
1 cup raw cashews
1 cup coconut cream
¼ teaspoon Red Boat Salt or kosher salt
2 tablespoons Red Boat Palm Sugar
1 tablespoon tapioca starch or cornstarch
2 mangoes, peeled, pitted, and sliced

Make the rice

1. Place the sweet rice and 2 quarts water in a large mixing bowl. Use your hands to swirl the rice around in the water to evenly saturate the rice. Soak the rice for at least 2 hours at room temperature, or overnight in the refrigerator.
2. Drain the water and refill the bowl with 2 quarts of clean water. Stir the rice to loosen any remaining starches, drain, and repeat until the water from the rice runs clear. Place the rice in a colander and let drain for 10 minutes.
3. To cook the rice, you can use a rice cooker or a steamer:

   RICE COOKER METHOD: Place the rice in the bowl of the rice cooker. Add 1 cup of water and cook using the sweet rice setting.

   STEAMER METHOD: Line the bottom of a steamer basket with clean cloth, like a bandana, then spread the rice in one even layer on the cloth. Steam the rice, covered, for 1 hour. After steaming, take the pot off the heat and keep the rice in the steamer until ready to serve.

Roast the cashews and make the coconut sauce

4. While the rice cooks, preheat the oven to 300°F. Place the cashews on a parchment-lined baking sheet, spreading them out evenly to ensure even roasting. Roast the cashews in the oven for 15 to 20 minutes, or until the nuts are aromatic and pale golden, then remove from the oven. When they're cool enough to handle, coarsely chop the nuts.
5. In a small saucepan over medium heat, bring the coconut cream, salt, palm sugar, and tapioca starch to a boil. Stir to melt the palm sugar with the cream. Bring to a boil for 2 minutes, then remove from heat and cool.

Assemble and serve

6. To serve, fan mango slices on each serving plate. Place a few spoonfuls of sticky rice alongside the mango slices, then top with the coconut sauce and a shower of chopped cashews.

BÁNH BÒ NƯỚNG (HONEYCOMB CAKE)

Coconut milk, palm sugar, and pandan are the foundation for this rich, fragrant cake that's perfect with tea. There actually isn't any honey in this recipe; rather, it's often called a honeycomb cake because the unique striations of its crumb resemble a honeycomb. This cake is a classic, and you've probably seen it at Vietnamese bakeries and delis—it's the wedge with a brown crust and, more often than not, a bright green interior. The cake is deceptively simple to make, but achieving that coveted honeycomb structure requires exact ingredients and an understanding of a few baking techniques.

First, unlike many of our other recipes, there is no substitute for palm sugar here. It is a must-have for this cake to shine. Second, the bright green color in many versions is accomplished by using pandan extract. We opted to sacrifice that color in order to use fresh (or frozen) pandan leaves, which have floral, almost vanilla-like notes and are available at your local Asian market. Third, because double-acting baking powder—the most common type of baking powder at supermarkets—has the potential to cause the cake to collapse, we do as my mother did and use single-acting baking powder. It can be slightly tricky to find, as many supermarket chains carry only double-acting baking powder; your best bet is to seek it out at the Asian market, too. Popular brands, in telltale pink sachets, are Alsa and IHA. Fourth, when combining the ingredients, we

→ *continued*

pass the eggs through a sieve and discard the thick membrane (called chalaza) for a smooth batter free of the air bubbles that would hinder the development of the interior structure. Finally, we use a 12-cup Bundt pan for a well-risen, evenly baked cake. When selecting your Bundt pan, choose one with a simple design: This will make turning out the cake much easier than one with intricate details.

MAKES 1 BUNDT CAKE

- **1** cup Red Boat Palm Sugar
- **1** (14-ounce) can coconut milk
- **½** cup roughly chopped pandan leaves, defrosted if frozen
- **¼** teaspoon Red Boat Salt or kosher salt
- **7** eggs, beaten
- **¼** teaspoon pure vanilla extract
- **½** cup rice flour
- **1½** cups tapioca starch
- **2½** teaspoons single-acting baking powder
- **2** tablespoons butter, softened to room temperature

1. Place a 12-cup Bundt pan in a cold oven, then preheat the oven to 340°F.
2. In a medium pot, combine the palm sugar, coconut milk, pandan leaves, and salt. Over medium heat, bring the mixture to a simmer.
3. Take the pot off the heat and stir to dissolve the sugar and salt. Set the pot aside and let the pandan leaves steep in the coconut milk for 20 minutes.
4. Strain the coconut mixture into a large mixing bowl. Squeeze the pandan leaves to extract as much liquid as possible, then discard them.
5. Place a sieve over the coconut mixture. Pass the eggs through the sieve and into the bowl, pressing the eggs against the sides of the sieve until all the whites and yolks are strained, leaving only the sinewy chalaza behind. Use a spatula to scrape the eggs clinging to the underside of the sieve into the bowl. Discard the chalaza.
6. Add the vanilla extract to the bowl and stir to combine.
7. In a separate mixing bowl, combine the rice flour, tapioca starch, and baking powder. Carefully sift the dry

ingredients into the coconut milk mixture. Gently stir to incorporate the flours into the coconut milk, then press the mixture through a sieve to break up any clumps of dough. Stir to incorporate into a smooth batter.

8. With oven gloves, carefully remove the Bundt pan from the oven. Working quickly and carefully, add the butter and coat just the bottom of the pan—avoid getting butter up the sides of the pan, or the cake will not rise properly. Pour the batter into the pan, then return the pan to the middle rack of the oven.

9. Bake for 30 minutes, then pierce a toothpick into the center of the cake. If there are bits of batter sticking to the toothpick, then the cake is still raw and needs more time. Bake for up to 10 more minutes, until the toothpick comes out clean.

10. Remove the pan from the oven and set it upside down over a wire rack to cool.

11. Once the cake is cool, use a thin butter knife to pry the edges away from the pan until the entire cake releases from the cake pan. Return the cake right-side up, slice into wedges, and serve. Note that the cake will begin to dry out in an hour, so immediately store any leftovers in an airtight resealable bag or container. It's best eaten within a day.

NICOLE KRASINSKI'S PALM SUGAR MOCHI CAKES

Nicole Krasinski is the co-owner and pastry chef at State Bird Provisions, one of our favorite restaurants, and The Progress, both in San Francisco. Her desserts are stunning—bursting with bright, layered flavors and a wonderful way to end any meal. Here she uses our palm sugar to make springy mochi cakes topped with strawberries and cream. Note that mochi flour is also called sweet rice or glutinous rice flour at the market. Any leftovers can be tightly wrapped and placed in an airtight container on your counter for up to two days.

SERVES 16

¼ cups plus **2** tablespoons Red Boat Palm Sugar
1¼ cups coconut milk
½ cup crème fraîche
¼ cup butter, melted and cooled
2 eggs
1 egg yolk
2 teaspoons vanilla extract
1¼ cups mochi flour
1 teaspoon baking powder
1 teaspoon kosher salt

FOR SERVING

2 pints fresh strawberries, washed and quartered
1½ cups heavy cream, whipped

1. Preheat the oven to 350°F. Line a 9-inch cake pan with parchment paper, and pan spray or butter the parchment. In a blender, combine the sugar, coconut milk, crème fraîche, butter, and eggs and egg yolk and blend until smooth.
2. In a bowl, combine the vanilla, flour, baking powder, and salt and whisk to combine. Add the wet ingredients to the dry and whisk to combine.
3. Pour the batter into the prepared pan. Bake for 40 to 50 minutes, until the cake is golden brown. Allow to cool, then remove from the pan. Cut into wedges and serve warm or at room temperature with fresh strawberries and whipped cream.

PALM SUGAR POWER

Not too long after I launched Red Boat, I was on a trip through Cambodia and passed by a few farms selling freshly made palm sugar by the bucket. Curious, I pulled over to give it a try. I was amazed: Creamy and slightly thicker than peanut butter, the flavor of the palm sugar was almost too good to be true. The sugar was sweet, but the sweetness wasn't monotonous—there were also deep, lush undertones of caramel and toasted nuts. It was unlike any other palm sugar I had tasted in the US. I brought some back to my family, and my uncles marveled over it, saying it brought them back to their childhoods. I know if my mother were alive then, she would have loved it.

On my next trip to Việt Nam, I took a detour to Cambodia, this time specifically to visit farms and research the process of making palm sugar. I learned that many farmers plant the trees along the perimeter of their rice fields; during the rainy season, the rice is harvested and the trees used as shade. During the dry season, workers tap the trees and collect the sap. From there, the sap is poured into huge shallow pans placed over fire, brought to a boil, and cooked down until it's about the consistency of condensed milk. It's then poured into buckets and sold to markets and passersby like me along the roadside.

I was so obsessed with this palm sugar that I decided to see if I could bring it to the US. I connected with a few family-owned farms making especially good sugar from a tree called thốt nốt, or palmyra palms, which is a tree indigenous to Cambodia and so culturally significant that it is one of the country's national symbols. Around 2013, we sourced enough to import to the US, and we began selling the palm sugar on our website. Since then, our palm sugar has become a sleeper hit among Red Boat's fans, as well as a favorite for those looking for sustainable, low-glycemic sugar alternatives. We do our best to keep it in stock, but, as with any natural product, its availability is heavily dependent on the weather. We actually couldn't get any palm sugar for a period of almost two years because of an unusually long rainy season! Nonetheless, when we do have it, it's a real treat for us and our Red Boat family.

If you do pick up a jar, I encourage you to try using it in desserts like our Bánh Bò Nướng (page 246), or in Nicole Krasinski's delicious Palm Sugar Mochi Cakes (page 250). However, it truly shines in kho. The foundation of the braise, of course, is a sauce made of caramelized sugar and oil. While you can certainly use granulated sugar to make the caramel sauce, swapping it out for palm sugar will transform the dish. The palm sugar bumps up all the aromatics, and as the braise reduces, the sugar's natural nutty, smoky flavors concentrate and intensify. The result will be a kho with a dimension of richness and complexity that you can't get from granulated sugar alone. That's the power of palm sugar.

SALTED MEYER LEMON SODA

This salted Meyer soda is a take on the beloved soda chanh muối, the salted lemonade soda found in restaurants, bakeries, and street stalls throughout Việt Nam. It makes for a refreshing drink anytime of the year, but it is downright essential during sweltering summer days. To make the lemonade, we start by salting and preserving the lemons (recipe follows). It takes three months, but that investment of time is worth it—once made, they'll last indefinitely. Feel free to swap out a little bit of carbonated water with a few splashes of gin or vodka to take this drink from lunchtime to cocktail hour.

SERVES 1

¼ cup Salted Meyer Lemons (page 254)

3 tablespoons granulated sugar

1 cup carbonated water

1. Add the salted lemons, along with their juices, to a large glass. Add the sugar.
2. Use a pestle or spoon to muddle the lemon and sugar until the sugar dissolves.
3. Add ice and carbonated water. Stir to combine. Serve immediately.

SALTED MEYER LEMONS

Meyer lemons made their way to the United States from Beijing, and we love them because they are more flavorful than most of the more common, thicker-skinned Eureka lemons. With less pith than Eurekas, they're also less bitter and smoother on the palate. Here we preserve the lemons in a brine that includes Red Boat Salt and chiles (the chiles introduce more warmth than spice and provide a nice counterpoint to the sweet-tart of the lemons). Although not necessary, the addition of citric acid helps the lemons attain a jelly-like chew that many salted-lemon aficionados love. Licorice root, often paired with citrus in Vietnamese preserves, lends an herbal complexity and is worth seeking out. If you're lucky enough to get your hands on a supply, try this technique with calamansi or Nagami kumquats.

MAKES 1 QUART

1¼ pounds Meyer lemons
½ pound coarse sea salt
¼ cup Red Boat Salt
Citric acid (optional)
1 tablespoon finely minced Thai chiles
5 grams sliced licorice root (5 to 10 slices, depending on size) (optional)

1. Wash and dry the Meyer lemons in a colander. Transfer to a large mixing bowl. Add the coarse salt.
2. Using your hands, rub the sea salt against the lemons. The coarse salt will act as a gentle abrasive on the lemons, removing the bitter essential oils from the skin. Scrub the lemons for 30 minutes. The salt should take on a faint yellow tint, indicating that the essential oils have been extracted from the lemon peels.

3. Remove the lemons from the salt and transfer to a colander. Rinse the lemons under running water and rub away any large salt granules, then transfer them to a large bowl of clean water. Set the lemons aside for 10 minutes to remove any residual salt. Return them to the colander and set aside to dry completely.
4. While the lemons are drying, prepare a brine: Combine the Red Boat Salt and ¾ cup water in a pot. Bring the brine to a boil, then remove the pot from the heat. Let the brine cool completely. Once the brine is cool, stir in a pinch of citric acid, if using.
5. Once the lemons are dry, pack them into a quart jar. Add the minced chiles and, optionally, the licorice root.
6. Pour the cooled brine into the jar. Place a tiny dish or ramekin inside the jar to keep the lemons submerged in the brine.
7. Cover and set aside in a cool place for at least 3 months before using.

BLOODY MARY

From the sweetness of the tomatoes to that kick of spice from the horseradish and hot sauce, the best Bloody Marys have layers and layers of flavor. Our version of this classic brunch cocktail includes a bit of fish sauce, which intensifies the umami in the other ingredients, especially the tomatoes. Indeed, this Bloody Mary relies on good tomatoes to stand up to the fish sauce and the other spices and seasonings in the drink. For that reason, we like to use super ripe, deeply flavorful heirloom tomatoes when they're in season. You can find them at specialty grocers or your local farmers market—look for the ones that seem just about ready to burst. If heirlooms aren't in season, canned or very ripe tomatoes will do, too.

SERVES 2

½ pound heirloom tomatoes
½ rib celery
¼ cucumber, peeled
1 teaspoon grated horseradish
2 teaspoons Red Boat Fish Sauce
2 teaspoons lemon juice
2 teaspoons Sriracha
1 teaspoon stone ground mustard
1 tablespoon minced parsley
4 shiso leaves
4 ounces vodka

1. In a blender, combine all the ingredients except the vodka and blend until smooth.
2. Add ice to two glasses. Pour 2 ounces of vodka and half of the blender mix into each glass.
3. Stir and serve.

MICHELADA

Fish sauce and tomatoes are two umami-rich ingredients, so when you put them in the same dish—or drink—the level of umami hits a whole other level. Here we add our fish sauce to bursting ripe tomatoes and combine them with the refreshing acidity of limes and the spice of Tajín to make our version of a michelada. This recipe is just enough for two, but you can scale it up and make a big pitcher for a party.

SERVES 2

1 pound ripe tomatoes, quartered
1 tablespoon plus 1 teaspoon Red Boat Fish Sauce
1 tablespoon Cholula Hot Sauce
Juice from 2 limes, half a juiced lime reserved (seeds removed)
Tajín or chili-lime seasoning
Ice
1 bottle Modelo or other light pilsner or lager

1. Combine in a blender the quartered tomatoes, fish sauce, Cholula, and lime juice. Blend until smooth.
2. Run the juiced lime half along each of two glass rims, then dip the rims into the Tajín to create a salt rim. Fill each glass with ice, add half of the michelada mix, and top with beer. Serve.

OUR NEW OLD-FASHIONED

With just sugar, bitters, and whiskey, the old-fashioned is one of the simplest cocktails. Our take on this classic is just as bare, with one twist: In place of sugar, we use a simple syrup made with our Red Boat Palm Sugar. Its warm notes of caramel and toasted nuts complement the bourbon and rye well. You'll make more syrup than you'll need for this recipe, so store any remaining in an airtight container in the fridge and try adding it in your other favorite cocktails, too.

MAKES 1 COCKTAIL

¼ ounce (1 teaspoon) Palm Sugar Simple Syrup, plus additional to taste (recipe follows)

2 to **3** dashes bitters

2 ounces bourbon or rye

Ice

GARNISH

Orange peel

1. Into a Collins glass, pour the simple syrup and bitters and stir well to combine. Pour the whisky into the glass and stir. Taste. If you'd like it sweeter, add up to ½ teaspoon more syrup.
2. Add ice cubes and stir to chill the cocktail. Twist the orange peel over the drink to release its oils, then slide it into the glass as garnish. Serve.

PALM SUGAR SIMPLE SYRUP

MAKES ABOUT ¼ CUP

2½ tablespoons Red Boat Palm Sugar

1. Place the palm sugar and 2 tablespoons of water in a small pot over very low heat.
2. Swirl the palm sugar in the water until the sugar has dissolved and liquid has thickened slightly, just a few minutes.
3. Immediately remove the pot from the heat. Once cooled, it's ready to use. Store any unused syrup in a jar or other airtight container, covered, in the fridge for up to 1 month.

CHAPTER 10

PICKLES, CONDIMENTS & MASTER STOCKS

PICKLES

Pickled Green Mango

Green Peppercorns

Red Boat Salt-Pickled Daikon and Carrots

Pickled Shallots

PICKLED CABBAGE

MAKES 1 QUART

For this pickle, we ferment cabbage in a rice-and-salt brine, rather than using vinegar as the souring agent. How long the cabbage ferments will depend on the flavor you're going for—we start tasting it on the fourth day, when the cabbage has a distinct but gentle sourness. By the sixth day, that sourness and tang will be more pronounced. If you let the cabbage continue to ferment after that, the flavors will deepen and the leaves will become soft and lose their crisp. Once it hits the level of sourness and texture you like, stick the jar in the fridge and use it within two weeks. This method can be used to pickle bean sprouts and green tomatoes as well.

3 tablespoons sweet rice
⅓ cup granulated sugar
1 tablespoon plus **1** teaspoon Red Boat Salt or kosher salt
½ pound cabbage
4 scallions, green tops only

1. In a mixing bowl, combine the sweet rice with 3 cups of water. Stir to rinse the rice. Soak the rice for 30 minutes, then drain and discard the water.
2. Transfer the rice to a tea sachet or tie it up in cheesecloth and place in a quart-size mason jar. Set aside.
3. In a medium pot, combine 2⅔ cups water, sugar, and salt and bring to a boil. Boil for 5 minutes. Set the brine aside to cool completely.
4. Cut and discard the core from the cabbage. Cut the cabbage leaves into 2-inch squares, then place in 1 gallon of water.
5. Add the scallion tops to the cabbage leaves. Agitate the cabbage and scallions in the water to loosen any bits of dirt clinging to the vegetables. Set aside to soak for 15 minutes.
6. Gently lift the cabbage and scallions from the water. Try not to disturb the water too much; doing so will bring up any dirt that's settled on the bottom of the bowl. Dry the cabbage and scallions well in a salad spinner or with paper towels, then pack them into the mason jar.
7. Once the brine is completely cool, pour it into the jar. Screw the lid tightly and place the jar in a dry place on your counter.
8. After a day or two in the brine of rice water and fish salt, small bubbles

will appear in the liquid, which is a good sign that the fermentation process has started. Let the cabbage continue to ferment for 4 to 7 days, unscrewing and tightening the lid once a day to release the gas in the pickle. On the fourth day, give it a try: If it's not sour enough to your liking, continue fermenting (and releasing the gas) for up to 3 more days. At that point, the pickle can remain on your counter, where it will continue to ferment and develop flavor. Alternatively, you can transfer the jar to the refrigerator to slow down the fermentation process.

RED BOAT SALT-PICKLED DAIKON AND CARROTS

MAKES ABOUT 1 QUART

Red Boat Salt adds a layer of complexity to the classic Vietnamese pickle of carrots and daikon. If you don't happen to have any of our salt in your pantry, you can, of course, use kosher salt instead. Whichever salt you use, make a big batch. This is, after all, a universal pickle: It goes well with most everything. And if you have some shallots on hand, you can use this recipe to pickle those, too.

⅓ cup granulated sugar
¼ cup plus **3** tablespoons white vinegar
2½ teaspoons Red Boat Salt or kosher salt
⅔ pound daikon, peeled and sliced into 4-inch-long matchsticks
¼ pound carrots, peeled and sliced into 4-inch-long matchsticks
¼ pound onion, thinly sliced

1. In a medium saucepot, combine ⅓ cup water, the sugar, vinegar, and salt. Bring the brine to a boil, then take the pot off the heat and cool for 10 minutes.
2. Add the vegetables to the slightly cooled brine. The daikon and carrots will start to soften in the brine within 5 minutes; at that point, gently mix in the vegetables.
3. Transfer the vegetables and their brine to a jar and cover. The pickles are ready to eat in an hour, but the flavor will improve the longer it sits. Any leftovers (or pickled shallots) will last, covered, in the fridge for 2 weeks.

PICKLED KOHLRABI AND CARROTS

MAKES ABOUT 1 PINT

Dishes like bún chả (page 153) are often accompanied with pickled green papaya and carrots, but because green papayas can sometimes be difficult to source here, we often use kohlrabi instead. A vegetable in the Brassica family, kohlrabi is slightly sweeter than the more neutral papaya but has a similarly crunchy texture. It's a terrific companion to smoky grilled meats. Of course, if you do have access to green papaya, feel free to use it here, too.

⅓ cup granulated sugar
2½ tablespoons vinegar
2 tablespoons Red Boat Fish Sauce
¼ pound kohlrabi, cored, peeled, and cut into ¼-inch matchsticks
¼ pound carrots, cut into ¼-inch matchsticks

1. In a small saucepot, combine ⅓ cup water, sugar, vinegar, and fish sauce. Bring the mixture to a boil. Set aside to cool.
2. Place the kohlrabi and carrots in a pint-size glass jar. Once the fish sauce brine has cooled, pour it over the vegetables. Let the vegetables pickle for 2 hours before eating. Any leftovers can be stored, covered, in the fridge for 2 weeks.

PICKLED GREEN MANGO

MAKES 1 QUART

This pickled mango is a great accompaniment to grilled or fried foods. You can use any variety of mango for this pickle, but when you're shopping, choose very firm green, unripe mangoes. Mangoes that are ripe, or even just starting to ripen, will not do, as they'll be too soft and won't give you that distinctive snap of a proper pickle. You can find green mangoes in many produce sections, and especially the produce sections in Southeast and South Asian grocery stores. And if you can source them, fresh green peppercorns also will pickle beautifully using this method (just omit the chiles).

½ cup Red Boat Fish Sauce
¾ cup granulated sugar
½ cup vinegar
1¼ pounds unripe mangoes
1 teaspoon minced Thai chile, ribs and seeds removed if desired
2 garlic cloves, minced
2 tablespoons minced ginger

1. In a medium pot, combine the fish sauce, sugar, vinegar, and 1 cup water. Bring the mixture to a boil and boil for 5 minutes. Remove the pot from the heat and let the brine cool to room temperature.
2. Meanwhile, peel the mangoes and remove their pits. Cut the mangoes into matchsticks or wedges.
3. Pack the mango into a quart-size mason jar. Add the chile, garlic, and ginger to the jar.
4. Pour the cooled brine into the mason jar. Cover, then place in the refrigerator. The pickle is ready to eat in 3 hours, but its flavor will improve after the mango sits in the brine for 24 hours. The pickle will keep, covered and refrigerated, for at least 2 weeks.

FISH SAUCE–PICKLED RADISHES

MAKES 1 QUART

Most Vietnamese pickles for everyday use are made with salt. But on special occasions like the Lunar New Year, fish sauce is used instead of salt. This not only gives the pickles a depth of flavor that salt alone could never do, it also helps cut the richness of all the other special-occasion food you're eating that day. These pickles are also delicious on their own. We use daikon here, but you can use any other variety of radish.

2 cups turbinado or granulated sugar
1 cup vinegar
¾ cup Red Boat Fish Sauce
2 garlic cloves, minced
2 Thai bird chiles, seeds and ribs removed if desired, minced (optional)
1 pound daikon
2 cilantro roots or 1 tablespoon coriander seeds
1 small white onion, thinly sliced

1. To make the brine, combine the sugar, vinegar, fish sauce, and ¼ cup of water in a pot and bring to a boil. Add the garlic and chiles, if using, and set the brine aside.
2. Wash and scrub the radishes to remove any grit. Remove their stems and slice the radishes into ¼-inch coins. Set aside.
3. If using cilantro roots, smash the roots with the blade of your knife to release their flavor. If using coriander seeds, leave them whole.
4. Pack the radishes, onion, and cilantro roots (or coriander seeds) into a large glass jar and pour in enough of the warm brine to cover the vegetables. Pickles are ready to eat after a day of brining.

For a crunchier and more toothsome pickle, before brining, place the sliced radishes on a baking sheet and slide them into a cold oven with the pilot light on and leave them overnight. This provides just enough heat to dry out the radishes. Alternatively, you can use a food dehydrator: Set the temperature to 110°F and let the radishes dehydrate for 4 hours.

Calamansi Nước Chấm

Nước Chấm Gừng (Ginger Dipping Sauce)

All-Purpose Nước Chấm

Mắm Nêm Pha (Unfiltered Anchovy Dipping Sauce)

NƯỚC CHẤM SPECTRUM

Like many Southeast Asian countries, Việt Nam has an entire universe of fish sauce–based sauces. In the US—and in this book—these sauces are known generally as nước chấm, but in Việt Nam, they also are known as nước mắm chua ngọt ("sour and sweet fish sauce") or nước mắm pha ("mixed fish sauce"). Under those umbrella terms, there are even more specific names for the dipping sauces, which often indicate the standout ingredient (nước mắm gừng, for example, is ginger fish sauce), or the dish they're paired with.

The best nước chấm strikes a delicate balance between the saltiness of the fish sauce with sweetness, acidity, spice, and, occasionally, fat. In the following pages, we offer recipes for nine different nước chấm. Which one to use and when? Here's a quick guide.

NƯỚC CHẤM	DESCRIPTION	USAGE AND PAIRING SUGGESTIONS
All-Purpose Nước Chấm Điệp Pham's Nước Chấm	Balanced	Dipping, rice seasoning, salad dressing—everything! Make a small batch of each and see which one you prefer.
Chef Khanh Ngo's Nước Mắm Trộn Gỏi (Fish Sauce Salad Dressing)	Similar to the All-Purpose Nước Chấm and Điệp Pham's Nước Chấm, but with more body	Salad dressing
Calamansi Nước Chấm	Exceptionally aromatic and refreshing with pronounced citrus notes	Fresh seafood
Nước Chấm Gừng (Ginger Dipping Sauce)	Warm and slightly sweet, ideal for livening up more delicate, gentle flavors	Poultry Sea snails, squid, octopus, and other mollusks Whole fried fish Simply prepared dishes, such as boiled meats and steamed vegetables
Peanut-Coconut Nước Chấm	Nutty, with a thick consistency	Dipping
Nước Chấm Me (Tamarind Dipping Sauce)	Punchy acidity, jammy, fruity with a hint of sourness	Heavily spiced foods Beef Pork
Mắm Nêm Pha (Unfiltered Anchovy Dipping Sauce)	Assertive brininess	Beef Seafood

MAKE YOUR OWN SIGNATURE NƯỚC CHẤM

To make nước chấm, you need fish sauce plus three, maybe four, additional ingredients: something sweet, something acidic, something spicy, and, if you want, something fatty. Because it's so endlessly customizable and highly personal, anyone who makes nước chấm regularly eventually comes up with their own signature version. And that version becomes a point of pride: To be considered the best nước chấm maker in your family or group is a badge of honor—and also the spark for some (mostly) friendly competition as others seek to dethrone the master.

If you want to experiment with making nước chấm with our Red Boat Fish Sauce, here's a quick primer. Start with that bottle, then choose an ingredient from each category at right. Note the ingredient suggestions in each category are just that: suggestions. Nước chấm can vary widely and, in Việt Nam, many nước chấm are region-specific and use local ingredients. You can do the same and use any unique ingredient local to you.

After choosing your team of ingredients, combine them in the proportions in our All-Purpose Nước Chấm recipe (page 275). This is a ratio, so if you increase the quantity of one ingredient, you'll have to increase the others, too. This is especially important when it comes to the acid, as a little bit goes a long, long way; if you add too much, you'll be forced to adjust all the other ingredients upwards, too . . . and you might end up with a tub of nước chấm, when you really intended to make just a cup. We suggest adding the acid last, in very small increments.

Once you're happy with your signature nước chấm, make a big batch, ladle some into jars to share with family and friends, and tuck the rest away in your fridge. Nước chấm made with vinegar will last at least a week. Nước chấm made with the juice of limes or other citrus will lose its aroma and flavor over time, so while it will keep for up to a week, it is its very best the day, and the day after, it's made. And if you really fall into the rabbit hole of experimenting with various types of nước chấm, try swapping out our fish sauce for a bottle of our Red Boat Mắm Nêm. Our Red Boat Fish Sauce is the liquid that remains after draining and straining the liquid from the barrels; the Mắm Nêm, on the other hand, is unfiltered, resulting in a cloudy liquid that is pungent and more intense than our fish sauce.

Start With
Water and Red Boat Fish Sauce

Choose Something Sweet

When dissolving the sugar is necessary, whisking it in rather than stirring will create a thicker sauce.

Granulated sugar
Palm sugar
Coconut water
Coconut soda
7Up
Pineapple*

+ Something Aromatic

For even more flavor, blanch the aromatics in boiling water to release their flavorful oils.

Minced garlic
Minced ginger
Minced lemongrass

+ Something Spicy

Minced or sliced chiles
Sriracha
Sambal oelek

+ (A Little Bit of) Something Acidic

White distilled vinegar
Apple cider vinegar
Tamarind
Fresh lime juice**
Fresh Calamansi juice**

(+ optionally) Something Fatty

Chopped peanuts or other fatty nuts
Sesame seeds
Shredded coconut

*Pineapple is sweet and acidic, so adjust your proportions of the other ingredients accordingly.

**Limes and calamansis are acidic and aromatic, so you may have to adjust the proportions of the other ingredients accordingly. They'll lose their aroma and vibrancy quicker than the other acids, so it's best to use nước chấm made with these citruses within a week.

CHUNKS
IN SYRUP
2019 HARVEST

ALL-PURPOSE NƯỚC CHẤM

FOR THE FRIDGE

Whenever you need a nước chấm, you can't go wrong with this one. As the name suggests, this nước chấm is so versatile that we always have a jar of it in our fridge. Use it as a dipping sauce for egg rolls, for example, or toss it with rice noodles in a salad. It's also great simply spooned over rice with grilled pork chops or chicken.

MAKES 1¼ CUPS

¼ cup Red Boat Fish Sauce
1 tablespoon vinegar
⅔ cup granulated sugar
1 garlic clove, minced
1 to **2** Thai chiles, seeds and ribs removed if desired, minced

1. Combine the fish sauce, vinegar, sugar, and 1 cup water to a small sauce pot. Bring mixture to a boil.
2. Take the pot off the flame and add minced garlic and chiles.
3. Chill in the refrigerator until ready to use. The nước chấm can be stored, covered, in the fridge for at least 1 week.

ALL-PURPOSE NƯỚC CHẤM

FOR ONE (OR FORTY)

Sometimes you need to make just enough nước chấm for one, sometimes you need to make it for a big party. In that case, the fail-safe way to make nước chấm is to rely on a ratio rather than specific measurements for the ingredients. The ratio is also a handy starting point if you're experimenting with the many different ways you can make nước chấm and need some guidelines on how to combine your selected ingredients (see page 273 for more on how to make your own custom nước chấm). So, whether you're measuring everything out with a small spoon or a teacup, the following will help you make exactly how much you need.

7 parts granulated sugar
1 garlic clove, smashed
1 to **2** Thai chiles, seeds and ribs removed if desired, chopped (optional)
12 parts hot water
4 parts Red Boat Fish Sauce
1 part distilled, white, apple cider, or champagne vinegar, or lime juice
Chopped peanuts (optional)

1. Combine the sugar, smashed garlic, and chopped chiles in a jar. Add hot water and stir to dissolve the sugar. Let this mixture steep for 15 minutes to allow the garlic and chiles to release their oils.
2. Add the fish sauce and vinegar. (If using lime or other citrus juice, make sure the water has completely cooled before adding; otherwise, the warm liquids may cause the juice to become bitter.) Stir to combine. Add the peanuts, if using.
3. The nước chấm can be used right away, but its flavor will improve the next day. Nước chấm made with vinegars will last at least 1 week in the fridge, and those made with lime juice are best used within the week they're made.

ĐIỆP PHAM'S
NƯỚC CHẤM

My sister makes her nước chấm with fresh lemon juice, which is a mellower acid than lime juice. It's another all-purpose nước chấm we love; try it anytime you need a dipping sauce for Vietnamese dishes.

MAKES ABOUT 2 CUPS

1¼ cups granulated sugar
1 cup Red Boat Fish Sauce
¾ cup fresh lemon juice or **½** cup apple cider vinegar
2 cloves garlic, finely minced (optional)
1 Thai chile, sliced

1. Place the sugar and fish sauce in a small pot set over low heat. Bring to a gentle boil and stir until all the sugar dissolves.
2. Remove the pot from the stove and add 1 cup of water and the lemon juice. Stir to combine, then add the garlic and chile pepper. Serve. Store any leftovers, covered, in the refrigerator for up to a week.

CHEF KHANH NGÔ'S NƯỚC MẮM TRỘN GỎI (FISH SAUCE SALAD DRESSING)

In the early days of Red Boat, when our California staff consisted of just me and whomever in my family I could harangue into helping me at the time, I frequently drove down to Little Saigon to deliver fish sauce to independently owned stores and distributors. These frequent trips to Orange County meant that I could catch up with my uncle Võ Trần and friends Huong and Khanh Ngô. They've provided a lot of emotional support for my then-nascent company, which I've always appreciated. Khanh is a chef and at her catering company, KDN Gourmet, she makes all sorts of delicious Vietnamese dishes. I especially love her salads, and this recipe is her "master recipe," she says, for salad dressing. It's terrific over any bowl of greens.

MAKES ABOUT 1 CUP

½ cup Red Boat Fish Sauce
½ cup granulated sugar
½ cup freshly squeezed lime juice
4 red jalapeños, seeds removed, finely minced
1 tablespoon freshly minced garlic

1. In a bowl, combing the fish sauce, sugar, and lime juice and stir until the sugar dissolves.
2. Stir in the chiles and garlic.
3. Use immediately, or store, covered, in the fridge for up to 1 week.

CALAMANSI NƯỚC CHẤM
(CALAMANSI DIPPING SAUCE)

Calamansi is a citrus similar in size to a lime, but quite different in taste. They're sweeter and more floral than limes, with incredibly fragrant oils. The juice from calamansis lends this nước chấm the same sort of tartness lime juice would, with an additional layer of sweetness. We source calamansis from farmers at our local farmers market; they also may be found at Filipino markets. As calamansis ripen, they go from green to orange—either may be used for this dipping sauce. It's especially great with fresh seafood.

MAKES ¾ CUP

1 Thai chile, minced
1 garlic clove, minced
¼ cup granulated sugar
2 teaspoons calamansi juice
2 tablespoons Red Boat Fish Sauce

1. Using a mortar and pestle, grind the chile and garlic with the sugar to release their oils, then transfer to a small bowl. Alternatively, if you're short on time, you can simply place all three in the bowl and mix to combine.
2. Stir in the Calamansi juice and fish sauce. Serve. Store any leftovers in an airtight container in the fridge. It's best used within a day or two.

NƯỚC CHẤM GỪNG

(GINGER DIPPING SAUCE)

This nước chấm bursts with the warmth and slight sweetness of ginger. It pairs especially well with poultry and simply prepared dishes, like steamed vegetables or steamed fish. For a smooth sauce without clumps of ginger fibers, slice the ginger across the grain, so the pieces break down more easily in the mortar.

MAKES ABOUT ½ CUP

¼ cup plus 2 tablespoons granulated sugar
3 tablespoons sliced ginger
1½ tablespoons smashed garlic
1 teaspoon chopped Thai chile
¼ cup Red Boat Fish Sauce
1 tablespoon lime juice

1. Add the sugar, sliced ginger, garlic, and chile to a mortar. Use a pestle to break down the spices and release the oils into the sugar. Once the ginger and garlic are completely broken down, remove the pestle. Stir the mixture for 5 minutes, until the sugar granules melt.
2. Add the fish sauce, lime juice, and ½ cup of water. Stir to combine. It's ready to use right away. Transfer any remaining nước chấm to an airtight container and cover. It will keep in the fridge for about 1 week.

PEANUT-COCONUT NƯỚC CHẤM

This nutty nước chấm is sweetened with coconut water and has an especially thick consistency thanks to the addition of ground peanuts. That unique consistency, in turn, makes it an ideal dipping sauce. Dunk a chicken wing or two (page 50) in it, for example, or serve it with rolls, as we do in our Phú Quốc Sardine Salad (page 57).

MAKES ABOUT 2 CUPS

¼ cup granulated sugar
2 to **4** Thai chiles, seeds and ribs removed if desired, chopped
1 tablespoon minced garlic
2 tablespoons Red Boat Fish Sauce
2 teaspoons lime juice
1 cup coconut water, from 1 to 2 mature coconuts (see page 59)
½ cup unsalted roasted peanuts, ground

1. Place sugar, 2 chiles, and garlic in a mortar. Grind the garlic and chiles until they disintegrate into the sugar. Transfer the chile-garlic mixture to a medium mixing bowl.
2. Add the fish sauce and lime juice. Using a fork, whisk the mixture until it starts to take on a sheen.
3. Add the coconut water and ground peanuts. Stir vigorously to combine.
4. Set the sauce aside until needed. Leftovers, if any, can be stored, covered, in an airtight container in the refrigerator for 5 days.

NƯỚC CHẤM ME

(TAMARIND DIPPING SAUCE)

Tamarind paste, made from the pods of the tamarind tree, is jammy and fruity, with a strong hint of sourness as well. Its boldness and brightness shine through in this nước chấm, but because it is so forward, it has the potential to overwhelm delicate flavors. Accordingly, the sauce is best paired with dishes that can stand up to it, like heavily spiced foods or beef.

MAKES ABOUT 1 CUP

¼ cup tamarind paste (see page 25)
2 teaspoons grapeseed, canola, vegetable, or other neutral oil
2 tablespoons minced garlic
½ cup granulated sugar
¼ cup Red Boat Fish Sauce
1 teaspoon minced Thai chile

1. Put the tamarind in a mixing bowl and pour in 1 cup hot water. Set aside to let the tamarind bloom.
2. Heat the oil in a sauté pan over medium heat. Add the minced garlic and sauté for 1 minute. Take the pan off the heat.
3. Set a strainer over a bowl. Strain the tamarind, pressing it into the strainer to extract as much liquid as you can from the tamarind. Discard the pulp.
4. Add ¾ cup of the tamarind juice to the garlic in the sauté pan. Bring the mixture to a boil over medium heat, then reduce the heat to low and simmer for 4 minutes.
5. Add the sugar, fish sauce, and chile to the sauté pan. Over medium heat, bring the mixture to a boil again, then reduce the heat to low and simmer for 4 minutes.
6. Take off the heat and cool before serving. It's ready to be used immediately. Store any leftovers, covered, in the fridge for up to a month.

MẮM NÊM PHA

(UNFILTERED ANCHOVY DIPPING SAUCE)

Mắm nêm is fish sauce before it undergoes the filtration process, and it has a flavor that is distinct from filtered fish sauce. While filtered fish sauce is light on the palate, mắm nêm is markedly brinier, with a more complex, oceanic sweetness. Most of our fish sauce is filtered, but we do bottle a limited amount of mắm nêm for fish sauce connoisseurs. This mắm nêm pha pairs well with beef and seafood.

MAKES ABOUT 1 CUP

1½ cups diced pineapple
2 teaspoons grapeseed, canola, vegetable, or other neutral oil
2 tablespoons minced lemongrass (see page 20 on how to mince lemongrass)
2 tablespoons minced garlic
1 teaspoon minced Thai chile
2 tablespoons Red Boat Fish Mắm Nêm (see page 18)
1 tablespoon granulated sugar

1. Set a strainer over a bowl. Squeeze the diced pineapple over the strainer, then put the pulp in the strainer to drain.
2. In a sauté pan over medium heat, heat the oil. Add the minced lemongrass and sauté until aromatic and toasted, about 1 minute.
3. Add the garlic and chile and sauté until aromatic, about 1 minute.
4. Add the pineapple pulp to the pan and sauté for 1 minute.
5. Add the mắm nêm, sugar, and strained pineapple juice. Bring the mixture to boil and cook for 3 minutes.
6. Transfer the mixture to a bowl and chill before serving. Leftovers can be stored, covered, in the fridge for about a month.

CILANTRO MAYONNAISE

Boosted with fish sauce and Maggi seasoning, this homemade mayonnaise will become a staple in your fridge. It's terrific as a spread for any sandwich, especially bánh mì.

MAKES 1⅔ CUPS

1 cup chopped cilantro stems
2½ teaspoons white distilled vinegar
1 teaspoon Red Boat Fish Sauce
1 teaspoon Maggi seasoning
1 teaspoon minced shallot
2 egg yolks
1 cup grapeseed, canola, vegetable, or other neutral oil

1. Add the cilantro stems, vinegar, fish sauce, Maggi seasoning, and shallot to a mason jar.
2. Use an immersion blender to grind the ingredients to a paste, about 1 minute.
3. Add the egg yolks and blend until smooth, about 1 minute.
4. With the blender motor running, slowly drizzle in the oil. Blend until all the oil is emulsified into a mayonnaise, about 2 minutes. Transfer the mayonnaise to a jar or other container and store for up to 4 days, covered, in the fridge.

RED BOAT SCALLION OIL

A jar of fragrant scallion oil is something we always, always have in the fridge. The oil is flavored by scallions and fish sauce, making it an ideal condiment to use on almost everything: Brush on some pork chops, try it with grilled fish. It's also great drizzled over a simple of bowl of steamed rice. When you're shopping for scallions to make this recipe, choose a bunch with long green tops, which are sweeter than the pungent white root ends. If you want to make a more delicate condiment, use only the green parts.

MAKES 1¾ CUPS

1 cup thinly sliced scallions, green and white parts

1 tablespoon Red Boat Fish Sauce

½ teaspoon granulated sugar

⅓ cup grapeseed, canola, vegetable, or other neutral oil

1. Place the scallions in a heatproof pint jar, then add the fish sauce and sugar.
2. In a small saucepan over medium heat, bring the oil to 180°F, which should take about 3 minutes.
3. Carefully pour the hot oil directly over the scallions. The scallions should sizzle once the oil is added.
4. Stir to combine all the ingredients. The scallion oil is now ready to use. To store, place the oil in an airtight container and refrigerate for up to 2 weeks.

ANNATTO OIL

Annatto oil has a subtly herbaceous fragrance and flavor, and because the oil has such a vibrant red hue, it's also used to add color to dishes. We use the oil fairly often in our cooking, so we've found it handy to have a batch stashed in the fridge. It takes just a few minutes for the rustic red annatto seeds to release their color into the oil, but do keep an eye on the flame: In those short minutes, the seeds can burn and turn the oil bitter if the temperature is too high.

MAKES ABOUT 1 CUP

1 cup grapeseed, canola, vegetable, or other neutral oil

¼ cup annatto seeds

1. In a small pan over medium heat, combine the oil and annatto seeds. Cook, stirring the annatto constantly, for 4 minutes. As the oil heats, the annatto will start to release its color.
2. After 4 minutes, turn off the heat and let the oil cool for 15 minutes.
3. Strain, discard the seeds, and store the oil, covered, in the refrigerator for up to 2 months.

LEMONGRASS CHILE OIL

Bursting with lemongrass, this chile oil was one of the signature condiments at Diep Tran's former restaurant, Good Girl Dinette. We start with ½ cup of chile flakes, which should be enough to give the oil a pleasant, slow-burning heat, but if you would like even more spice, tip in ⅔ cup of chiles instead. In either case, add a judicious dollop of the oil to soups and porridges, or a small spoonful to your nước chấm. The chile oil also pairs wonderfully with beef, tofu, and summer vegetables.

MAKES 2 CUPS

2 cups canola oil
2 cups minced lemongrass (see page 20 for tips on mincing lemongrass)
½ pound garlic, minced
½ to **⅔** cup chile flakes
⅓ cup granulated sugar, plus additional to taste
¼ cup Red Boat Fish Sauce, plus additional to taste

1. Pour the oil into a heavy-bottom pot. Over medium heat, bring it to 300°F on a deep-fry thermometer, or until a wooden chopstick placed into the oil starts to bubble. Carefully add the lemongrass and garlic and stir until the garlic starts to become lightly toasted and aromatic, 5 to 7 minutes. Lower the heat to the lowest flame and add the chile flakes. Stir to the saturate the chile flakes with the oil.
2. Add ½ cup of water and cook on low heat for 2 hours, stirring every so often to prevent the garlic from scorching at the bottom.
3. After 2 hours, take the oil off the heat and stir in the sugar and fish sauce. Taste the oil. Adjust and add more sugar or fish sauce if you wish. Store leftovers, covered, in the refrigerator for 3 months.

FRIED SHALLOTS AND SHALLOT OIL

A handful of fried shallots is often the finishing touch on porridge and many other dishes we make at home. You can always use store-bought shallots, but if you can spare the time, freshly fried shallots are crispier and more flavorful than most store-bought versions—plus, you'll gain the frying oil, which is beautifully fragrant and ready to be drizzled over steamed vegetables or a hot bowl of rice.

A few quick tips: Take the time to separate the shallots into individual rings, which will help to fry them evenly. Because shallots can burn very quickly, we highly recommend using a fry basket to give you better control as you fry. Alternatively, you can fry the shallots in batches using the largest metal strainer you have. Pull the shallots out of the oil just when they turn a light golden color. Once out of the fryer, the shallots will continue to cook, so by the time they're completely cooled, they'll be perfectly browned and crisped. Finally, make sure the shallots are cooled before transferring them to a jar. If the shallots are still warm, the residual heat will create steam and turn the shallots soggy.

MAKES ABOUT 1½ CUPS FRIED SHALLOTS AND 2 QUARTS SHALLOT OIL

1 pound shallots

2 quarts grapeseed, canola, vegetable, or other neutral oil

1. Peel the shallots and slice into ⅛-inch slices. Separate the slices into rings.
2. In a medium heavy-bottomed pot set over medium heat, heat the oil to 245°F on a deep-fry thermometer. The oil should be about 2 inches high, but should not be more than halfway up the pot.
3. Put the shallot rings into a fry basket, then lower the basket into the oil. The liquid from the shallots will cause the oil level to rise initially, but will subside as the shallots fry.
4. Fry the shallots for 2 minutes, stirring constantly. After 2 minutes, lift the fry basket. Hold the basket above the oil for 30 seconds to drain the excess oil from the basket, then lower the basket back into the oil. Repeat this fry, stir, lift, drain, lower process 3 to 5 times. During this time, the shallots will go from translucent to a light golden color, and constantly dipping the shallots in and out of the oil will help you monitor the shallots and avoid burning them. In total, this process should take between 7 and 13 minutes, depending on the moisture level of your shallots.
5. Once the shallots reach the desired color, drain and transfer them to a paper towel–lined wire rack set over a baking sheet.
6. Repeat with any remaining shallots.
7. Cool completely, then transfer the shallots to a jar. Carefully pour the shallot oil into a separate jar. Store the shallots in an airtight container in the pantry for up to 7 days; the oil will keep in the fridge for months.

CHICKEN STOCK

Homemade chicken stock is full of rich flavor and is hands down better than any commercially made stock. With fish sauce that lends a subtle, nuanced complexity, this is our go-to for almost every recipe that calls for chicken stock. If you want to make a large batch of stock, you can simply double or triple the ingredients. Just add enough water in step 3 to cover the chicken by 1½ inches.

MAKES 2 QUARTS

2½ pounds chicken backs, wings, and/or legs
2 teaspoons kosher salt
1 pound onion, quartered
2 teaspoons whole black peppercorns, or **2** Thai chiles
4 to **6** tablespoons Red Boat Fish Sauce, divided
8 scallions
1 ounce ginger

1. If using chicken backs, remove the kidneys. If using whole chicken legs, butcher the legs at the joint, separating the thigh from the drumstick. Add the chicken pieces, salt, and 4 quarts of cold water to a stockpot, then place the pot in the refrigerator. Let the chicken soak for at least an hour, or overnight.
2. Drain the water and refill the pot with more cold water. Swish the chicken around in the water to loosen any residual impurities sticking to the surface of the chicken, then drain the water again.
3. Add the quartered onion, black peppercorns or chiles, 2 tablespoons fish sauce, and 1 quart of cold water.

Over high heat, bring the pot to a boil. Skim the impurities that rise to the surface.

4. Reduce the heat to a low simmer. If large bubbles break the surface, the flame is too high; lower the heat so the surface of the water just trembles (about 200°F). Simmer the stock for 1½ hours.
5. Remove the onion and chicken. The joints should separate easily from the bones, which is a sign that the flavorful collagen in the bones have been released into the stock.
6. Turn off the heat and add the scallions and ginger to the pot. Cover the pot and steep them for 30 minutes.
7. Strain the entire broth through a fine mesh cloth. If the stock ends up being less than 2 quarts, add enough water to make up the difference.
8. Add 2 more tablespoons of fish sauce to the stock. Taste and add up to 2 additional tablespoons if you feel the stock isn't salty enough.
9. The stock can be used immediately, or you can freeze it for up to a year.

If you're short on time, the stock can also be made in a pressure cooker. The flavor won't be as delicate as a stovetop stock, but will be excellent nonetheless. After soaking and draining the chicken in steps 1 and 2, add the chicken, onion, peppercorns, fish sauce, and 1½ cups of cold water to the pressure cooker. Pressure cook for 15 minutes, then proceed with step 5.

PORK STOCK

We make our own pork stock often—it's that easy to do. This stock is meant for everyday use when you want pork flavor instead of chicken. Use meaty bones like knuckles, hocks, neck bones, leg bones, and back bones, as those have a combination of marrow, collagen, tendon, and fats that will yield a flavorful broth that is more complex than using bones alone. It's great, for example, in the Mushroom and Egg Cháo (page 38) and Wontons in Soup (page 166).

MAKES 2 QUARTS

- **1** tablespoon kosher salt
- **2½** pounds meaty pork bones
- **1** pound white or yellow onion, quartered
- **2** ounces peeled fresh ginger, sliced ½ inch thick
- **7** whole black peppercorns
- **5** to **6** tablespoons Red Boat Fish Sauce, divided
- **2** bunches scallions

1. In a large stockpot, bring 4 quarts water to a boil. While the water comes to a boil, prepare an ice bath by filling a large mixing bowl with water and ice.
2. When the water comes to a boil, add the salt and pork bones. Continue boiling for 10 minutes, then remove the bones and plunge them into the ice bath. Keep the bones submerged in water for 15 minutes, then scrub the impurities still clinging to the bones. Drain the cloudy water, refill the bowl with clean water, and scrub off any impurities remaining. Drain, refill, and scrub one more time.
3. Clean the pot you used to blanch the bones. Add 2½ quarts clean water and return the pork bones to the pot.

4. Add the onion, ginger, peppercorns, and 2 tablespoons of fish sauce to the pot. Bring the pot to a boil over high heat. Boil for 10 minutes, skimming any impurities that float to the surface, then lower the heat so the water is at a bare simmer—the water's surface should just tremble with the occasional bubble. Simmer for 4 hours.
5. After 4 hours, tug at a joint: It should release easily from the bone. If not, continue simmering, checking every 15 minutes until the bones release from the flesh.
6. Turn off the heat and add the scallions to the pot. Press them down to submerge them in the stock. Cover the pot and let the scallions steep in the residual heat for 30 minutes.
7. Strain the stock through a fine mesh cloth. If the stock ends up being less than 2 quarts, add enough water to make up the difference.
8. Add 3 tablespoons more of fish sauce to the stock. Taste and add another tablespoon if you feel the stock needs it.
9. The stock can be used immediately. Any leftovers can be frozen: Pour the stock into a few airtight containers, cool, then place in the freezer until needed. The stock will keep in the freezer for up to one year.

If you're pressed for time, the stock can also be made in a pressure cooker. After blanching the pork bones in step 2, add the bones and the rest of the ingredients to the pressure cooker. Add 1¾ quarts water and pressure cook for 1½ hours, then continue with the recipe at step 6.

FISH STOCK

This is a good way to use fish bones from the Butterflied Grilled Perch (page 121), but if you don't have any fish bones on hand, ask for some at your local fish market: Full-service counters often will sell the bones for next to nothing. Alternatively, pick out a whole fish rather than precut steaks and fillets. Ask the fishmonger to fillet it and save the bones for you—with very little effort and expense, you'll turn those leftover bones into a delicious fish stock ready to use in, say, our Seafood Chowder (page 135).

MAKES 2 QUARTS

2 pounds fish bones, including spines, heads, and fins

½ pound shallots, diced

½ teaspoon whole black peppercorns

1 stalk lemongrass

1 cup cilantro stems

3 to **4** tablespoons Red Boat Fish Sauce

1. Place the fish bones in a pot large enough to fit the bones snugly. Add the shallot and peppercorns.
2. Trim the lemongrass tops until you see the pink center. Discard the portion that was above this pink center. Halve the base lengthwise and use the back of your knife to bruise and smash the base, then add both halves to the pot.
3. Using the same knife technique, bruise and smash the cilantro stems, then add them to the pot.
4. Add 8 cups water. The water should cover the bones. Bring the pot to a boil, then reduce the flame to low and simmer for 20 minutes.
5. Turn off the heat and let the stock steep for another 10 minutes. Strain through a fine mesh cloth. Discard the solids.
6. Add 3 tablespoons fish sauce to the stock. If the stock ends up being less than 2 quarts, add enough water to make up the difference.
7. Taste and add up to 1 additional tablespoon of fish sauce if you feel the stock isn't salty enough. Use immediately or transfer to pint or quart containers and store in the freezer for up to one year.

BUTTERY SHELLFISH STOCK

This stock is redolent of the sea, making it the perfect base for seafood dishes like our Seafood Chowder (page 135) and Cháo Bồi (page 218). It's also a perfect way to use crab and shrimp shells, which you can stockpile in your freezer. Crack the crab shells into very small pieces so you can extract as much flavor as possible. The addition of butter not only gives the stock an extra dimension, it also serves to trap the flavors of both the shells and the aromatics before they evaporate. Note that crab and shrimp shells take a bit longer than fish bones to release their flavor. The wait is worth it.

MAKES 1 QUART

- **1¾** pounds crab shells, shrimp shells, or a mix of both
- **¼** cup butter
- **¼** pound white onion, chopped
- **1** Thai chile, halved, seeds and ribs removed
- **1** to **2** tablespoons Red Boat Fish Sauce

1. If using crab shells, place them in a heavy-duty plastic bag and smash them into smaller pieces using a rolling pin. Add the crab or shrimp shells to a tall, heavy-bottomed pot, along with the butter, onion, and chile.
2. Cook over medium heat to caramelize the shells and onion, about 15 minutes, stirring frequently to prevent the onions from burning.
3. Add 4 cups of water. The water should cover the bones and shells; if not, choose a more narrow pot. Bring to a boil, then lower the flame and simmer for 1 hour.
4. Strain the stock through a fine mesh cloth. Discard the solids. Add 1 tablespoon fish sauce. If the stock ends up being less than 1 quart, add enough water to make up the difference. Taste and add 1 more tablespoon of fish sauce if you feel the stock isn't salty enough.
5. Use immediately or cool and transfer to pint or quart containers and freeze for up to one year.

A DAY IN SÀI GÒN

Every time I'm in Phú Quốc, I make time to take the one-hour flight from the island to Sài Gòn. I grew up there and, while a lot has changed since I was a kid, I still love the city. And I especially love the food: At every hour of the day, there is something to eat or try, including specialties from vendors who have been in the same spot for decades. If you have just one day in Sài Gòn, and you want to spend it eating, I have just the itinerary for you:

7:00 A.M. COFFEE AT CÀ PHÊ VỢT

Every morning, a long, rambunctious line of mopeds idle in the alley where the tiny Cà Phê Vợt is located. Open since 1955, the coffee shop is one of very few left in Sài Gòn that brews fresh coffee using a net-like cloth as long as a knee-high sock (hence the name of the shop—literally, "net coffee"). The brew is strong and dark; whether hot or iced, ask for your cup with just a bit of condensed milk to cut the bitterness. You can sip your coffee on a nearby stool, or take a walk down to Nhà Thờ Tân Định, a Roman Catholic church built by the French in the late 1800s.You won't miss it. The church not only has dramatic Gothic elements in its architecture, its entire exterior is painted an outstanding shade of pink.

330/2 Phan Đình Phùng, Phú Nhuận District

8:00 A.M. BREAKFAST #1 AT BÚN MỌC THANH MAI

Bún mọc is a northern noodle soup that made its way to the south after Việt Nam was divided into two in 1956. With a clear pork and shiitake mushroom broth, it's exceptionally light, so it's great for breakfast. Thanh Mai started serving her bún mọc some forty years ago, when she

brought her soup in her gánh (a shoulder pole) and set down right here, on this corner. I first came by around 1989, on my aunt's recommendation; it was only 8:00 a.m., and I wasn't quite hungry yet, so I told her I'd swing back for breakfast. She warned me she'd be sold out in two hours. And sure enough, the buckets were dry by the time I circled back at 10:00 a.m. Thanh did so well over the years that she was able to move her operations from the street into the building just a few feet away. It's not easy to scale up without losing quality, but her soup is as good now as when she was ladling it from the gánh. She still sells out, so don't make my mistake: Get there early.
14 Trương Định, Phường Bến Thành, District 1

Just a few blocks away is Chợ Bến Thành, the largest, and one of the oldest, markets in Việt Nam, with vendors selling everything from food to fabrics to souvenirs. Musulman Mosque, the biggest mosque in Sài Gòn, and one of the most beautiful, is also a short stroll away. When you've worked up another appetite, grab a taxi and head to . . .

10:00 A.M. BREAKFAST #2 AT PHỞ TÀU BAY

I've been going to Phở Tàu Bay for comforting bowls of beef phở since I was kid, usually for breakfast or lunch. There are actually two sibling restaurants called Phở Tàu Bay, which opened in 1954 located right next to each other. If you're walking up to the two restaurants, I prefer the restaurant on the left, at 433 Lý Thái Tổ, where the workers wear yellow shirts. Ask for a bit of nước béo, or beef tallow, to keep your bowl warm, and an egg to crack into your phở.
433 Lý Thái Tổ, Phường 9, District 10

12:00 P.M.
LUNCH #1 AT BÚN RIÊU TÔM KHÔ

My old neighborhood has changed a lot over the decades, but what hasn't changed is Bún Riêu Tôm Khô. This stand was, and continues to be, just steps away from my childhood home and my elementary school, and I used to come here for crab noodle soup all the time after class. As it happens, the owner of the stand, Thanh, was a student in my mom's class, and it was her mom who started selling bún riêu here fifty-five years ago. Her version of bún riêu includes dried shrimp and thick slices of chả lụa, or Vietnamese ham, and is a great example of the many ways this soup can be made.

207 Nguyễn Kim, Phường 7, District 10

2:00 P.M.
LUNCH #2 AT BÁNH XÈO ĂN LÀ GHIỀN

If I land in Sài Gòn in the late afternoon, Bánh Xèo Ăn Là Ghiền is often my first stop. The bánh xèo here is excellent: The shell, made of turmeric and coconut milk batter, is the rare one that is so thin, so delicate, and so crisp that it shatters. Stuffed inside is a generous heap of bean sprouts, plump shrimp, and mushrooms. After you order, you can watch the skilled cooks make your bánh xèo before it's plated and served with lettuce, herbs, and nước chấm. *74 Đường Sương Nguyệt Anh, Phường Phạm Ngũ Lão, District 1.*

By this time, the afternoon heat and humidity may start to hang heavy in the air. It's a good time to head back to your hotel and take a nap.

6:00 P.M.
DINNER AT HAI LÚA OR BÒ KHO GÁNH

Hai Lúa, in Sài Gòn's Chinatown, is a huge, multilevel space popular for celebrations: birthdays, weddings, you name it. If you're traveling with a large group and feel like sitting down for a meal, Hai Lúa is the spot. Call ahead to reserve its most famous dish: suckling pig, served with fried buns. *648 Đường Nguyễn Trãi, Phường 11, District 5*

Alternatively, you can head back to District 10 for beef stew at Bò Kho Gánh. Bò Kho Gánh has been serving satisfying bowls of bò kho since 1975. Each table is outfitted with a basket full of fresh, ethereal bánh mì to dip into the stew. On my first visit there, I had two bowls in one sitting! But you might want to limit yourself to just one so you can take a walk around to work up another appetite: This neighborhood is full of amazing street food. *029 Lô H Chung Cư Ngô Gia Tự, Dường Sư Vạn Hạnh, Phường 2, District 10*

APPENDIX
MENU PLANNING

QUICK MEALS AND EASY DINNERS

On days you're short on time, mix and match from the following starters and mains to build a meal in no time:

STARTERS

MAINS

WEEKEND DINNERS AND PROJECTS

When you have the whole weekend to tend to the stove, or want to make an impressive centerpiece for a dinner party, the following fit the bill:

The Ultimate Thịt Heo Quay (Crispy Pork Belly) **page 156**
Mom's Gà Quay (Roast Chicken) **page 193**
Oxtail Soup **page 209**
Brisket Phở **page 206**
Bún Riêu (Crab Noodle Soup) **page 107**
Seafood Chowder **page 135**
Bún Kèn (Coconut Fish with Noodles) **page 140**
Thịt Ba Rọi Cuốn (Pork Roast) **page 159**

PICNIC-READY DISHES

These dishes travel well, making them ideal for a picnic or any other time you need to pack some food to go. For salads and sandwiches, pack the dressings, pickles, and spreads separately and assemble when you arrive at your destination.

Bacon and Egg Breakfast Bánh Mì **page 31**
Crab Rolls **page 132**
Red Boat Ginger-Cilantro Fried Chicken **page 187**
Bánh Bò Nướng (Honeycomb Cake) **page 246**

WRAP PARTIES

For big gatherings with friends or family, offer everything they need to make their own rolls. You'll need:

Herb platters (see page 18 on building an herb platter)
Assorted pickles
Assorted nước chấm
Lemongrass Chile Oil **page 288**
Fried Shallots **page 290**
Bánh tráng (rice paper wrappers; see page 17 for suggestions about shopping for bánh tráng)
Any one or a combination of:
Chả Giò Tôm Thịt (Imperial Rolls with Shrimp and Pork) **page 52**
Nem Nướng (Grilled Pork Meatballs) **page 149**
Chạo Tôm (Sugarcane Shrimp) **page 116**
Phú Quốc Sardine Salad **page 57**
The Ultimate Thịt Heo Quay (Crispy Pork Belly) **page 156**
Butterflied Grilled Perch (serve tortillas with this, too!) **page 121**

WHOLE30-FRIENDLY DISHES

With a few modifications (removing sugar where necessary, say, or replacing butter with a non-dairy alternative), the following dishes can be successfully made Whole30-friendly:

SALADS AND VEGETABLES

Rau Muống Xào (Morning Glory with Garlic) **page 78**
Broccolini with Very Delicious Garlic Sauce **page 76**

MAINS

Canh Chua (Pineapple Catfish Soup) **page 113**
The Ultimate Thịt Heo Quay (Crispy Pork Belly) **page 156**
Thịt Ba Rọi Cuốn (Pork Roast) **page 159**
Ann's Chicken Soup **page 179**
Ragu Gà (Chicken Ragu) **page 181**
Christine Hà's Laab (Thai Minced Pork Salad) **page 212**
Cà Ri Gà (Chicken Curry) **page 190**
Oxtail Soup **page 209**
Lẩu (Shrimp Hot Pot) **page 231**

INDEX

Note: Page references in *italics* indicate photographs.

hmhbooks.com

Library of Congress Cataloging-in-Publication Data

Names: Pham, Cuong (Chef), author.
Title: The Red Boat fish sauce cookbook : beloved recipes from the family behind the purest fish sauce / Cuong Pham ; with Tien Nguyen and Diep Tran.
Description: Boston : Houghton Mifflin Harcourt, [2021] | Includes index.
Identifiers: LCCN 2021014687 (print) | LCCN 2021014688 (ebook) | ISBN 9780358410973 | ISBN 9780358411499 (ebook)
Subjects: LCSH: Cooking, Vietnamese. | BISAC: COOKING / Specific Ingredients / Herbs, Spices, Condiments | COOKING / Individual Chefs & Restaurants
Classification: LCC TX724.5.V5 P48 2021 (print) | LCC TX724.5.V5 (ebook) | DDC 641.59597—dc23
LC record available at https://lccn.loc.gov/2021014687
LC ebook record available at https://lccn.loc.gov/2021014688

Book design by Sebit Min

Printed in China
SCP 10 9 8 7 6 5 4 3 2 1